Slimming Magazine was first published in 1969 and now has a readership of one and a quarter million. Year by year, *Slimming Magazine*'s reputation has grown as the world's leader in its field. This success is based on one editorial aim: to be the best friend a dieter ever had . . . a friend who is understanding, honest, sensible – and fun. And supremely well informed. *Slimming Magazine* is able to advise on diet and nutrition with all the authority of an internationally respected scientific team. Its very human experts also have an unrivalled insight in the everyday practical problems of dieting: they have suffered themselves!

Glynis McGuinness was senior home economist on *Slimming Magazine* for four years. She previously managed the executive directors' dining room at Thames TV, spent two years working in a special diets department of a hospital in Sydney, Australia and has worked as a home economist for Metal Box and Lyons Maid. She edits a number of *Slimming Magazine* booklets each year.

Sybil Greatbatch is deputy editor of *Slimming Magazine*. Before joining the magazine in 1978, she worked full time as an editor for BBC Publications while running a *Slimming Magazine Club* in her spare time. She has also edited *The Complete Dieting Revolution* (1981) and *Slimming: the Complete Guide* (1982).

Slimming Magazine's

Housewife's Diet Book

edited by Glynis McGuinness
and Sybil Greatbatch

Fontana Paperbacks

First published by Fontana Paperbacks 1983

Set in 10½ on 12½ Linotron Plantin
Made and printed in Great Britain by
William Collins Sons & Co. Ltd, Glasgow

Contents

Introduction

Maybe you have always been plump, but for many women getting married and having children is the start of their weight problem. Perhaps you enjoy showing off your culinary skills and serving your husband high-calorie cakes and pastries which you can't resist sampling. Pregnancy is often a great excuse to start eating for two and you may end up with an after-baby bulge you didn't bargain for. The increase in your weight could be very gradual, and it is not until you find that you've outgrown the larger size clothes which you bought last year that you have to face the prospect of buying an even bigger size, or doing something about your weight.

Being at home all day, either on your own or with young children to look after, creates special dieting problems which women who go out to work don't have to cope with. Cooking for the family can mean a daily battle with temptation. With other people in the household to consider it's not possible to keep your cupboards bare, and the proximity to a store of food for most of the day may be hard to handle. As nibbling can be one of the most common causes of failure to lose weight, we have included in this book a chapter on very low-calorie nibbles and snacks which will keep you munching all day if you wish.

In devising the recipes in this book we have tried to make your dieting campaign as easy as possible. We have kept breakfasts very simple as this is usually a busy time for anyone with a husband to get off to work and children to dispatch to school. We have devised lunches to be cooked for one, although they can be made in larger quantities if you have the children at home midday. We have included a chapter on convenience meals that can be shared with your husband or a friend, but the main section of the book concentrates on meals to serve to the family. When slimming there is absolutely no need to sit at the end of the dining table nibbling a lettuce leaf while you enviously watch your family tuck into a hearty meal. That way you'll end up feeling resentful that you have to slim while they can eat just what they like. And resentments of that sort often lead to secret raids on the biscuit tin!

Many delicious main meals can become low in calories if you change your method of cooking. Stop frying and adding fat to stews and casseroles and the calorie saving can be considerable. A small 25g (1 oz) knob of butter, or margarine counts for 210 calories. Because all the recipes in this book are low in fat, they follow the recommendation for good health endorsed by all modern nutritional experts. So by cooking for your family the low-fat way, you will be introducing them to a very healthy way of eating as well as helping yourself to lose weight. Many recipes are also high in fibre.

We have given vegetable portions separately as you may want to add additional vegetables to non-dieters' plates. If you use our handy measures, you can easily dish up your own calorie-controlled portions, allowing the family to eat whatever they need from what remains.

To follow main meals, we have devised some low-calorie puddings that can also be shared with others; and if you can't avoid baking cakes, there is a chapter which gives you the lowest calorie recipes you could attempt.

How to plan your dieting menus

To start with, you need to decide the number of calories you are going to allow yourself each day. A calorie is simply a unit of energy. Mrs Average uses up 700 calories a day doing the housework, going shopping, watching the television, doing the ironing, etc. Her body burns up a further 1400 calories just keeping all essential functions going, such as breathing, pumping round the blood and controlling body temperature. If every day Mrs Average eats 2100 calories she will keep her weight steady. If she eats more than this, the body will store any excess calories as fat to be used up another day. If the day never comes that she eats less than 2100 calories the fat store will remain. If Mrs Average eats less than 2100 calories her body will need to raid its larder of fat and she will lose weight. Not everyone, however, will burn up exactly the same number of calories as Mrs Average. If you are particularly active and exercise regularly you may well burn up more calories. If you are a lounge lizard you could burn up less.

Many people start a diet feeling they must limit themselves to 1000 calories a day. It is certainly not necessary to diet at a calorie total lower than this. But many women will lose weight if they diet on 1250 or even 1500 calories a day. The heavier you are, the more calories you need to just move your body from point A to point B; so if you have three stone or more to lose, then you should start your diet at 1500 calories and cut down the calories as you get slimmer. If you have one stone or under to lose you will need to keep to a strict 1000 calories as the last few pounds are often the most stubborn to shift. If you have been dieting for a long time you will probably also find that you need to keep to 1000 calories because your body tends to gradually adjust to taking fewer calories and stops burning them up quite so efficiently. Aim at around 1250 calories if you have between one and three stone to lose. For your ideal weight, check the chart on p. 12.

Having decided on your calorie total for the day, plan out in advance what you will eat. If you are cooking a meal for the family, then the starting point needs to be your main meal. Work out how many calories you will spend on this and calculate how many calories you have left for your remaining meals. The recipes in each chapter are given from the lowest to the highest in calories so you can easily pick out a meal for the calories you want to spend. The calorie chart at the back of this book gives the values of basic foods and drinks. You can drink as much black coffee, lemon tea, water and drinks labelled low-calorie as you wish; but remember to count into your allowance all calorie-containing drinks. If you have milk in tea and coffee your best plan is to measure your daily allowance into a jug and use it throughout the day. This way you won't need to measure every cup and won't be guessing at calories when you can't be bothered to measure.

If you keep your menus as varied as possible you will automatically be taking in all the nutrients and vitamins you require. Ensure that you do get some fresh vegetables and fresh fruit regularly.

Try to keep shopping to a minimum and buy only the things you intend to eat. Never go shopping on an empty stomach or you will probably find your basket full of foods you didn't intend to buy (and you'll be lucky if you get home without delving into a packet of biscuits or sweets). Decide now on the foods that tempt you most and ban them from the house for the period of your diet. If you explain to the family that you need their help in making one or two small sacrifices they may do a deal by settling for alternative food treats which are not as tempting for you.

Don't get resentful if the family is not totally helpful to begin with. How many times have you said you will diet and given up after a few days? It may take them a little while to get used to the idea that this time you are serious and have found the ideal way to lose weight. As the pounds start to disappear you will probably find the family will get more interested in your success and will want to help more. So get out your pen and paper and work out your diet plan for tomorrow. This time you are going to lose those excess pounds for good.

IDEAL WEIGHT CHART Here we provide a guide to your ideal weight – your proper poundage could be up to 7 lb either side of the medium-frame figure given for your height. Your mirror is the best judge of whether you have reached your ideal target weight. You are aiming at a covering that looks good and feels non-flabby.

What a Woman should weigh without shoes, allowing 2 to 3 lb (or about 1kg) for light indoor clothing

Height			Medium Frame
4-ft-10	1.47m	7-st-8	48kg
4-ft-11	1.50m	7-st-11	49.5kg
5-ft-0	1.52m	8-st-0	51kg
5-ft-1	1.55m	8-st-3	52.5kg
5-ft-2	1.57m	8-st-7	54kg
5-ft-3	1.60m	8-st-9	55kg
5-ft-4	1.63m	8-st-12	56.5kg
5-ft-5	1.65m	9-st-1	57.5kg
5-ft-6	1.68m	9-st-8	61kg
5-ft-7	1.70m	9-st-9	61.5kg
5-ft-8	1.73m	9-st-12	62.5kg
5-ft-9	1.75m	10-st-2	64.5kg
5-ft-10	1.78m	10-st-5	66kg
5-ft-11	1.80m	10-st-10	68kg
6-ft-0	1.83m	11-st-0	70kg

What a Man should weigh without shoes, allowing 2 to 3 lb (or about 1kg) for light indoor clothing.

Height			Medium Frame
5-ft-1	1.55m	8-st-11	56kg
5-ft-2	1.57m	9-st-1	57.5kg
5-ft-3	1.60m	9-st-4	59kg
5-ft-4	1.63m	9-st-7	60.5kg
5-ft-5	1.65m	9-st-10	62kg
5-ft-6	1.68m	10-st-1	64kg
5-ft-7	1.70m	10-st-5	66kg
5-ft-8	1.73m	10-st-9	67.5kg
5-ft-9	1.75m	10-st-13	69.5kg
5-ft-10	1.78m	11-st-4	72kg
5-ft-11	1.80m	11-st-8	73.5kg
6-ft-0	1.83m	11-st-12	75.5kg
6-ft-1	1.85m	12-st-3	77.5kg
6-ft-2	1.88m	12-st-8	80kg
6-ft-3	1.90m	13-st-0	82.5kg

Breakfasts

Breakfast can be a busy time for housewives, particularly those who have children to get off to school. Current research into eating habits of families shows that the traditional three-course cooked breakfast no longer graces the dining table in the majority of modern homes. And that's good news for all slimmers. Families often eat breakfast at different times, with the housewife preparing one breakfast for her husband before he leaves for work and another for the children before they go to school. She may decide to have her own breakfast when everyone has left and she can sit down and relax.

Most people tend to have a favourite breakfast that they eat day after day. First thing in the morning is not a good time for creative thinking! So we have kept breakfasts in this section simple and made them suitable for one person. You can, of course, serve them to the family as well, but their portions need not be strictly controlled.

Weigh and measure all your ingredients very carefully. Cereals in particular vary enormously in the amount you actually get in your dish for 25g (1 oz). You will find that you'll get far more cornflakes, for example, than muesli which weighs a lot heavier.

The breakfasts in this section start at 130 calories and go to 280 calories. If you are accustomed to having a big breakfast, we suggest you start with one of the more substantial breakfasts and try to bring your calories down gradually.

Eating can be strongly governed by habit and breakfast eating seems to be the most habit-governed meals of the day. But it is possible to change – and the lower in calories you make your first meal, the more calories you'll have for later.

If you're not in the habit of eating breakfast at all, please don't feel you have to start. Save your calories for later in the day or have a bowl of cereal when you most feel like eating.

Toast and Marmalade
Serves 1: 130 calories

1 slice bread from a large, medium-sliced loaf
7g (¼ oz) low-fat spread
5ml (1 level teaspoon) marmalade *or* honey *or* jam

Toast the bread and serve with the low-fat spread and marmalade or honey or jam.

Grapefruit, Boiled Egg and Crispbread
Serves 1: 155 calories

½ grapefruit
5ml (1 level teaspoon) sugar
1 egg, size 3

1 Energen *or* Crackerbread *or* Ryvita crispbread
5ml (1 level teaspoon) low-fat spread

Sweeten the grapefruit with the sugar. Boil the egg. Spread the crispbread with the low-fat spread and eat with the egg.

Cornflakes
Serves 1: 165 calories

25g (1 oz) cornflakes
5ml (1 level teaspoon) sugar
150ml (¼ pint) skimmed milk

Serve the cornflakes with the sugar and milk.

All-Bran and Banana
Serves 1: 175 calories

1 small banana
25g (1 oz) All-Bran
125ml (4 fl. oz) skimmed milk

Peel and slice the banana and serve with the All-Bran and skimmed milk.

Weetabix
Serves 1: 175 calories

2 Weetabix
5ml (1 level teaspoon) sugar
150ml (¼ pint) skimmed milk

Serve the Weetabix with the sugar and skimmed milk.

Flakes and Raisins
Serves 1: 175 calories

15ml (1 level tablespoon) raisins *or* sultanas
25g (1 oz) cornflakes *or* Kellogg's 30% Bran Flakes
150ml (¼ pint) skimmed milk

Sprinkle the raisins or sultanas over the flakes and serve with skimmed milk.

Muesli with Yogurt
Serves 1: 205 calories

25g (1 oz) muesli
1 small carton natural yogurt

Stir the muesli into the yogurt.

Weetabix with Dried Apricots
Serves 1: 210 calories

25g (1 oz) dried apricots
2 Weetabix
150ml (¼ pint) skimmed milk

Roughly chop the dried apricots and serve with the Weetabix and skimmed milk.

Krispies with Banana
Serves 1: 215 calories

1 small banana
25g (1 oz) Coco Krispies *or* Rice Krispies
150ml (¼ pint) skimmed milk

Peel and slice the banana and serve with the Krispies and skimmed milk.

Banana, Yogurt and Muesli
Serves 1: 240 calories

1 medium banana
1 small carton natural yogurt
30ml (2 level tablespoons) muesli

Peel and slice the banana and mix with the yogurt. Sprinkle the muesli on top.

Sausages and Baked Beans
Serves 1: 240 calories

2 chipolata sausages
150-g (5.3-oz) can baked beans with tomato sauce

Grill the chipolata sausages well. Heat the baked beans and serve with the sausages.

Baked Beans on Toast, and Juice
Serves 1: 240 calories

150-g (5.3-oz) can baked beans with tomato sauce
1 slice bread from a large, medium-sliced loaf
125ml (4 fl. oz) unsweetened orange *or* grapefruit juice

Heat the baked beans. Toast the bread and serve the beans on top. Drink the juice.

Shredded Wheat
Serves 1: 245 calories

2 Shredded Wheat
10ml (2 level teaspoons) sugar
150ml (¼ pint) skimmed milk

Serve the Shredded Wheat with the sugar and skimmed milk.

Muesli
Serves 1: 250 calories

50g (2 oz) muesli
125ml (4 fl. oz) skimmed milk

Serve the muesli with skimmed milk.

Grapefruit, Toast and Marmite
Serves 1: 280 calories

½ grapefruit
5ml (1 level teaspoon)
  sugar
2 slices bread from a large,
  medium-sliced loaf

15g (½ oz) low-fat spread
10ml (2 level teaspoons)
  Marmite *or* Bovril *or*
  yeast extract

Sweeten the grapefruit with the sugar. Toast the bread and spread with low-fat spread and Marmite, Bovril or yeast extract.

Light Lunches for One

If you have to cook a meal for the family in the evening, you probably won't go to a lot of trouble at midday. So we have devised these light meals to be quick and easy to prepare. If the children come home to lunch, then you may well find that they are quite happy to have the same as you if you choose something like Fish Fingers and Baked Beans or one of the Toasties.

You will find in this chapter frozen individual-portion meals and canned items. Keep some of these in your freezer or storecupboard at all times so that you always have a low-calorie meal available. Then you'll never break your diet with the excuse that you can't be bothered to decide what to eat or to go out to buy it.

When you're at home all day, nibbling can be a problem. So if this is one of your downfalls, make sure that you choose a low-calorie breakfast and one of the first lunches in this chapter (calories range from a saintly 145 to a more substantial 415). You will then be able to afford one or even two items from the chapter on Very Low-Calorie Snacks, whenever you feel the nibbling urge strike.

You will notice in the following recipes that we don't use butter or margarine to spread on bread or crispbreads. Low-fat spread is half the calories of any make of butter or margarine (even margarine high in polyunsaturates) so the calorie saving can be considerable. You could try serving a low-fat spread, such as St Ivel Gold or Outline, to your family. Don't tell them what it is and you may find that they don't notice the difference! Many fillings and toppings are moist enough without a fatty spread. The more good habits you get your family converted to now, the easier will be your task in staying slim later.

Bacon Steak with Pineapple
Serves 1: 145 calories

1 bacon steak, 100g (3½ oz)
1 ring pineapple, canned in natural juice, drained
125g (4 oz) mushrooms
5ml (1 level teaspoon) mustard

Grill the bacon steak. Place the pineapple ring on top of steak and grill until hot. Poach mushrooms in water. Serve with bacon and mustard.

Fish Cakes with Tomato Ketchup
Serves 1: 165 calories

2 fish cakes
15ml (1 tablespoon) tomato ketchup
125g (4 oz) frozen runner beans

Grill the fish cakes without any added fat. Boil the beans and serve with fish cakes and tomato ketchup.

Soup with Savoury Crispbreads
Serves 1: 150 calories

295-g (10.4-oz) can Heinz SlimWay Low-Calorie Soup, Chicken and Vegetable *or* Scotch Broth	2 Krispen crispbreads 10ml (2 level teaspoons) Marmite *or* Bovril *or* yeast extract 1 triangle cheese spread

Heat the soup. Spread the crispbreads with Marmite or Bovril or yeast extract and the cheese spread. Serve with the soup.

Prawn Salad
Serves 1: 150 calories

75g (3 oz) shelled prawns 30ml (2 tablespoons) Waistline Seafood Sauce lettuce	cucumber watercress celery green *or* red pepper

Mix the prawns with the seafood sauce and serve with as many of the salad vegetables as you want.

Tuna Salad
Serves 1: 160 calories

100-g (3½-oz) can tuna in brine
2 tomatoes
lettuce
cucumber
spring onions
celery
radishes
15ml (1 tablespoon) Waistline Seafood Sauce

Drain the tuna. Quarter the tomatoes. Place tuna and tomatoes on a plate with as much lettuce, cucumber, spring onions, celery and radishes as you like. Serve with the seafood sauce.

Poached Egg on Toast
Serves 1: 165 calories

1 egg, size 3
1 slice bread from a large, medium-sliced loaf

Poach the egg. Toast the bread and serve poached egg on toast.

Mushrooms and Cheese on Toast
Serves 1: 175 calories

1 slice bread from a large,
   medium-sliced loaf
5ml (1 level teaspoon)
   Marmite *or* Bovril
213-g (7½-oz) can
   mushrooms in brine

1 Kraft Cheddar *or*
   Cheshire Singles Cheese
   Slice

Toast the bread and spread with Marmite or Bovril. Drain
the mushrooms well, and then place on top. Grill for a few
moments to heat through. Cover with the cheese slice and
grill until melted and bubbling.

Ham and Corn Relish Crispbreads
Serves 1: 180 calories

40g (1½ oz) lean cooked
   ham
¼ red *or* green pepper
45ml (3 level tablespoons)
   corn relish

3 Energen *or* Krispen
   crispbreads

Discard all visible fat from the ham, then chop the lean.
Discard white pith and seeds from the pepper and dice the
flesh. Mix with ham and corn relish and spread on the
crispbreads.

Cod in Cheese Sauce
Serves 1: 185 calories

individual packet Findus Cod in Cheese Sauce
125g (4 oz) frozen broccoli

Boil the cod in cheese sauce in its bag as directed. Cook the broccoli in the same pan for the last 5 minutes and serve with the fish.

Cottage Cheese and Fruit Salad
Serves 1: 190 calories

50g (2 oz) grapes
1 medium peach *or* 1 small
   orange
lettuce

113g (4 oz) carton Eden
   Vale Cottage Cheese
   with Pineapple

Halve and pip the grapes. Halve and stone the peach and cut into large cubes; or peel and segment the orange. Arrange some lettuce on a plate and pile the cottage cheese in the middle. Surround with the fruit.

Tuna with Coleslaw Salad
Serves 1: 195 calories

100g (3½ oz) can tuna in brine
142g (5 oz) carton St Ivel Coleslaw in Low-Calorie
   Dressing

Drain and flake the tuna and serve with the coleslaw.

Beefburgers
Serves 1: 200 calories

2 Findus Beefburgers
2 tomatoes
15ml (1 level tablespoon) tomato ketchup

Thoroughly grill the beefburgers. Grill the tomatoes and serve with beefburgers and tomato ketchup.

Cottage Cheese and Olive Crispbreads
Serves 1: 205 calories

113-g (4-oz) carton Eden Vale Cottage Cheese with
   Onion and Peppers
3 Energen Brancrisp *or* Crackerbread *or* Ryvita
   crispbreads
2 stuffed olives

Spread cottage cheese on the crispbreads. Slice the olives and arrange on top.

Grilled Trout
Serves 1: 210 calories

1 trout, 175g (6 oz)   125g (4 oz) frozen peas
5ml (1 level teaspoon)   few sprigs watercress
   chopped parsley   1/4 lemon

Grill the trout without added fat. Sprinkle the parsley on top and serve with watercress, lemon and peas.

Banana and Cottage Cheese Open Sandwich
Serves 1: 210 calories

1 slice bread from a large, medium-sliced loaf
50g (2 oz) Eden Vale Cottage Cheese with Pineapple
1 small banana

Spread the bread with cottage cheese. Slice the banana and
arrange on top.

Roast Beef with New Potatoes and Brussels Sprouts
Serves 1: 220 calories

1 individual pack Ross Gravy with Roast Beef
125g (4 oz) frozen Brussels sprouts
125g (4 oz) drained canned new potatoes

Cook the roast beef and Brussels sprouts as instructed.
Heat the potatoes and serve with the meat and sprouts.

Herring with Tomato Chutney
Serves 1: 225 calories

1 small herring, 130g (4½ oz)
125g (4 oz) runner beans, fresh or frozen
15ml (1 level tablespoon) tomato chutney

Grill the herring without any added fat. Boil the beans and
serve with the herring and tomato chutney.

Battered Cod
Serves 1: 230 calories

1 Birds Eye Oven Crispy Cod Steak
125g (4 oz) Birds Eye Peas and Baby Carrots
15ml (1 tablespoon) tomato ketchup
vinegar

Cook the cod as instructed, then drain on kitchen paper. Boil the vegetables and serve with the cod, tomato ketchup and a little vinegar.

Steaklet with Relish
Serves 1: 230 calories

1 Birds Eye Steaklet
2 tomatoes
15ml (1 tablespoon) Bicks Relish, any flavour

Grill the steaklet well and grill the tomatoes. Serve with the relish of your choice.

Plaice with Tartare Sauce
Serves 1: 230 calories

150g (5 oz) fillet plaice
8 sprays Limmits Spray & Fry
125g (4 oz) frozen mixed vegetables
15ml (1 level tablespoon) Waistline Tartare Sauce
1/4 lemon

Spray the plaice with Spray & Fry, then grill. Boil the vegetables. Serve with the plaice, tartare sauce and the lemon.

Fish Cakes and Peas
Serves 1: 235 calories

2 fish cakes	15ml (1 tablespoon)
125g (4 oz) frozen peas	tomato ketchup
1 medium pear *or* peach	

Grill the fish cakes without any added fat. Cook the peas as instructed on the packet and serve with fish cakes and tomato ketchup. Follow with the pear or peach.

Steak and Kidney Pancakes with Coleslaw
Serves 1: 235 calories

2 Findus Steak and Kidney Savoury Pancakes
227g (8 oz) Eden Vale Coleslaw in Vinaigrette

Bake the steak and kidney pancakes without any added fat, at 190°C (375°F), gas mark 5, for 15 minutes and serve with the coleslaw.

Chicken with Peach and Chutney
Serves 1: 235 calories

1 chicken breast, 175g (6 oz)	125g (4 oz) frozen broccoli
1 canned peach half, drained	15ml (1 level tablespoon) mango chutney

Grill the chicken breast and then discard the skin. Grill the peach half for the last minute or until heated through. Boil the broccoli. Serve with the chicken, peach and mango chutney.

Cod in Shrimp Flavour Sauce
Serves 1: 240 calories

1 pack Birds Eye Cod in Shrimp Flavour Sauce
125g (4 oz) Birds Eye Peas, Sweetcorn and Peppers

Boil the fish in the bag as instructed. Add the vegetables
to the pan for the last 5 minutes. Drain and serve with the
fish.

Sausage, Bacon and Tomatoes
Serves 1: 240 calories

2 rashers back bacon
1 pork chipolata
2 tomatoes

Thoroughly grill the bacon and the sausage. Grill the
tomatoes and serve with the bacon and sausage.

Casserole with Vegetables
Serves 1: 245 calories

1 packet Findus Broad Oak Casserole
125g (4 oz) frozen mixed vegetables

Cook the casserole as instructed. Boil the vegetables and
serve with the casserole.

Cheesy Pancakes
Serves 1: 250 calories

2 Findus Cheddar Cheese Pancakes
2 tomatoes
15ml (1 tablespoon) bottled brown sauce

Bake the pancakes without any added fat at 190°C (375°F), gas mark 5, for 15 minutes. Cut the tomatoes in half and cook alongside the pancakes for the last 5 minutes. Serve the pancakes and tomatoes with the sauce.

Spicy Egg Crispbreads plus Orange
Serves 1: 250 calories

1 egg, size 3
15ml (1 level tablespoon)
   Waistline Spicy
   Vegetable Low-Calorie
   Spread

4 Energen Brancrisp *or*
   Ryvita Crispbreads
1 medium orange

Hardboil the egg and then cool in cold water. Shell, chop and mix with the low-calorie spread. Spread on the crispbreads. Follow with the orange.

Pot Rice
Serves 1: 255 calories

1 carton Golden Wonder Savoury Beef Pot Rice

Make up the pot rice with boiling water as instructed.

Scrambled Eggs on Toast
Serves 1: 255 calories

2 eggs, size 3   salt and pepper
30ml (2 tablespoons)   1 slice bread from a large,
   skimmed milk   medium-sliced loaf

Lightly beat eggs with the skimmed milk and season with salt and pepper. Cook over a gentle heat in a non-stick pan, stirring all the time, until creamy. Toast the bread and serve the scrambled eggs on top.

Bacon and Eggs
Serves 1: 260 calories

2 rashers back bacon
1 egg, size 3
little oil

Grill the bacon until the fat is crisp. Fry the egg in oil and then drain well and serve with the bacon.

Fruit and Nut Sandwich
Serves 1: 260 calories

1 small banana   1 walnut half
5ml (1 level teaspoon)   2 slices bread from a large,
   raisins *or* sultanas   medium-sliced loaf

Mash banana and mix with raisins or sultanas and chopped walnut. Use bread to make into a sandwich.

Cod in Cheese Sauce with Mixed Vegetables
Serves 1: 265 calories

170-g (6-oz) pack Findus Cod in Cheese Sauce
125g (4 oz) frozen mixed vegetables
1 medium apple *or* pear

Cook the fish as instructed and add the vegetables to the
pan for the last 10 minutes of cooking time. Serve the
vegetables with fish in sauce. Follow with the apple or
pear.

Ravioli au Gratin
Serves 1: 265 calories

215-g (7.6-oz) can Heinz Ravioli with Savoury Tomato
  Sauce
15g (1/2 oz) Edam cheese
30ml (2 level tablespoons) fresh breadcrumbs

Heat the ravioli gently in a small pan and then turn into
a small ovenproof dish. Grate the Edam and sprinkle on
top of the ravioli with the breadcrumbs. Grill until the
topping starts to brown.

Sweet and Sour Drumsticks
Serves 1: 270 calories

3 chicken drumsticks
½ packet Colman's Sweet
and Sour Sauce

150ml (¼ pint) water
125g (4 oz) bean sprouts,
fresh or canned

Grill the drumsticks then discard the skin. Lightly boil or heat bean sprouts. Make up the sauce mix using the water and serve with the drumsticks and bean sprouts.

Sausages and Beans
Serves 1: 275 calories

2 pork chipolata sausages
25g (1 oz) Branston-type pickle
150-g (5.3-oz) can baked beans in tomato sauce

Grill the sausages well, heat the beans and serve with the pickle.

Bacon and Beans on Toast
Serves 1: 275 calories

1 rasher back bacon
150-g (5.3-oz) can baked beans with tomato sauce
1 slice bread from a large, medium-sliced loaf

Grill bacon until crisp. Heat the beans and toast the bread. Serve beans on the toast and top with bacon.

Mixed Grill
Serves 1: 275 calories

1 Findus Beefburger
1 pork chipolata
1 rasher streaky bacon
1 lamb's kidney

125g (4 oz) mushrooms
5ml (1 level teaspoon)
  mustard *or* 15ml (1
  tablespoon) brown sauce

Grill the beefburger, chipolata sausage and bacon thoroughly. Grill the kidney. Poach the mushrooms in water and serve with the mixed grill and mustard or brown sauce.

Soup plus Snackpot Supreme
Serves 1: 280 calories

1 sachet Batchelor's Slim-a-Soup *or* Carnation Slim
  Soup, any flavour
1 pot Batchelor's Snackpot Supreme

Make up the soup and the snackpot as instructed.

Cheesy Baked Potato
Serves 1: 280 calories

175g (6 oz) potato
113-g (4-oz) carton St Ivel Cottage Cheese with Onion
  and Cheddar
salt and pepper

Scrub the potato, then bake in the oven at 200°C (400°F), gas mark 6, for about 45 minutes or until soft when pinched. Cut in half lengthways and carefully scoop out the flesh leaving the shells intact. Mash the flesh with the cottage cheese and season with salt and pepper. Pile back into the cases and reheat in the oven for 10–15 minutes.

Note You could bake the potato the day before when cooking the family meal to save fuel. Store filled potato in refrigator, then re-heat for 15-20 minutes.

Smoked Haddock with Bread
Serves 1: 280 calories

1 pack Findus Smoked Haddock, 170g (6 oz)
1 slice bread from a large, medium-sliced loaf
7g (¼ oz) low-fat spread

Cook the smoked haddock as instructed. Spread the bread with the low-fat spread and serve with the fish.

Ham and Tomato Sandwich
Serves 1: 280 calories

2 slices bread from a large,   25g (1 oz) lean cooked
   medium-sliced loaf   ham
15g (½ oz) low-fat spread   1 tomato

Spread the slices of bread with low-fat spread. Discard all visible fat from the ham and slice the tomato. Use to make a sandwich.

Chicken Supreme
Serves 1: 280 calories

1 pack Birds Eye Chicken Supreme
125g (4 oz) frozen peas

Cook the Chicken Supreme as instructed. Boil the peas and serve with the chicken.

Ham and Coleslaw plus Yogurt
Serves 1: 280 calories

50g (2 oz) lean ham
227-g (8-oz) carton Eden Vale Coleslaw in Vinaigrette
1 small carton St Ivel Prize Fruit Yogurt *or* 1 small
    carton Eden Vale *or* St Michael Natural Yogurt

Discard any visible fat from ham and serve with coleslaw. Follow with yogurt.

Baconburgers with Corn Relish
Serves 1: 285 calories

2 Birds Eye Baconburgers
25g (1 oz) Bicks Corn Relish
2 tomatoes

Grill the baconburgers thoroughly. Grill the tomatoes and serve with the baconburgers and corn relish.

Prawn Curry
Serves 1: 285 calories

1 pack Birds Eye China Dragon Prawn Curry
25g (1 oz) rice

Cook the prawn curry as instructed. Boil the rice and serve with the curry.

Chicken Breast with Mushroom Sauce
Serves 1: 285 calories

1 chicken breast, 175g (6 oz)	150ml (¼ pint) skimmed milk
½ packet Colman's Mushroom Sauce Mix	125g (4 oz) Birds Eye Cauliflower, Peas and Carrots

Grill the chicken breast, then discard the skin. Boil the vegetables. Make up the mushroom sauce mix with the skimmed milk and serve with the chicken and vegetables.

Sole and Asparagus with Vegetables
Serves 1: 290 calories

1 pack Young's Sole and Asparagus Royale
125g (4 oz) frozen runner *or* French beans
213-g (7½-oz) can mushrooms in brine

Cook the Sole and Asparagus Royale and the green beans as instructed. Heat the mushrooms, drain and serve with the fish and beans.

Fish Fingers and Spaghetti
Serves 1: 290 calories

3 fish fingers
215-g (7.6-oz) can spaghetti in tomato sauce

Grill the fish fingers without any added fat and serve with
the heated spaghetti.

Cheeseburger
Serves 1: 295 calories

1 Findus Beefburger	15ml (1 level tablespoon)
1 bap, 50g (1¾ oz)	Bicks Hamburger
1 Kraft Cheddar Singles	Relish *or* tomato
Cheese Slice	ketchup

Grill the beefburger well. Split the bap and toast the cut
sides. Place the beefburger on one half of the bap and top
with the cheese slice. Grill until cheese melts. Top with
hamburger relish or tomato ketchup and place other half
of bun on top.

Cod with Parsley Sauce
Serves 1: 300 calories

175g (6 oz) cod fillet	½ packet Colman's
8 squirts Limmits Spray &	Parsley Mix
Fry	125g (4 oz) frozen peas
150ml (¼ pint) skimmed	
milk	

Squirt the cod with the Spray & Fry then grill. Boil the
peas. Make up the sauce mix with the skimmed milk and
serve with the cod and peas.

Chicken and Mushroom Casserole
Serves 1: 305 calories

1 packet Birds Eye Chicken and Mushroom Casserole
125g (4 oz) Birds Eye Peas and Baby Carrots
1/2 medium packet Smash

Cook the chicken and mushroom casserole and the peas and baby carrots as instructed. Make up the Smash and serve with the casserole and vegetables.

Chicken Curry
Serves 1: 305 calories

283-g (10-oz) can Crosse & Blackwell Chicken Curry and Rice
15ml (1 level tablespoon) mango chutney

Heat the chicken curry as instructed and serve with the mango chutney.

Braised Kidneys with Mash
Serves 1: 305 calories

1 pack Birds Eye Braised Kidneys
1/2 medium packet Cadbury's Smash

Cook the kidneys as instructed. Make up Smash as instructed without any added butter and serve with kidneys.

Beef Pancakes with Baked Beans
Serves 1: 310 calories

2 Birds Eye Minced Beef Savoury Pancakes
150-g (5.3-oz) can baked beans with tomato sauce

Bake the pancakes without added fat at 190°C (375°F), gas mark 5, for 15 minutes. Heat the baked beans and serve with the pancakes.

Fish Fingers and Baked Beans
Serves 1: 310 calories

3 fish fingers
150-g (5.3-oz) can baked beans with tomato sauce
1 medium apple

Grill fish fingers without any added fat. Heat the baked beans and serve with fish fingers. Follow with the apple.

Chicken Leg and Bacon
Serves 1: 315 calories

1 chicken leg joint, 225g (8 oz)
1 rasher streaky bacon
125g (4 oz) sweetcorn, frozen or canned

Grill the chicken leg joint and then remove the skin. Crisply grill the bacon. Boil or heat the sweetcorn. Serve with the chicken and bacon.

Rump Steak
Serves 1: 320 calories

175g (6 oz) rump steak   watercress
125g (4 oz) mushrooms
5ml (1 level teaspoon)
  mustard

Trim any excess fat from the rump steak and grill it until medium or well cooked. Poach mushrooms in water and serve with the steak, mustard and watercress.

Ravioli and Ham Au Gratin
Serves 1: 320 calories

25g (1 oz) lean cooked   15g (½ oz) Cheddar cheese
  ham   15ml (1 level tablespoon)
215-g (7.6-oz) can Heinz   fresh breadcrumbs
  Ravioli with Savoury
  Tomato Sauce

Discard all visible fat from the ham and chop the lean. Mix with ravioli and heat through gently in a saucepan. Turn into an ovenproof dish. Grate the cheese and sprinkle on ravioli with the breadcrumbs. Grill until cheese melts.

Liver, Bacon and Beans
Serves 1: 325 calories

75g (3 oz) lamb's liver
8 squirts Limmits Spray &
  Fry

150-g (5.3-oz) can baked
  beans
1 rasher streaky bacon

Squirt the liver with the Spray & Fry and then grill.
Crisply grill the bacon and serve with the liver.

Soup and Bread plus Pudding
Serves 1: 325 calories

283-g (10-oz) can Crosse & Blackwell Farmhouse Thick
  Vegetable Soup
1 slice bread from a large, medium-sliced loaf
1 Chambourcy Flanby Caramel

Heat the soup and serve with the unbuttered bread.
Follow with the Flanby Caramel.

Buck Rarebit
Serves 1: 330 calories

1 egg, size 3
1 slice bread from a long, medium-sliced loaf
40g (1½ oz) Lancashire cheese

Poach the egg. While it is poaching, toast the bread on one
side only. Grate or crumble the cheese and place on the
untoasted side. Grill until melted and starting to turn
brown. Serve the egg on top.

Lasagne and Green Salad
Serves 1: 330 calories

1 Birds Eye Lasagne, 250g spring onions
(9 oz) cucumber
lettuce 30ml (2 tablespoons)
watercress oil-free French dressing
green pepper

Cook the lasagne as instructed. Make a green salad with the lettuce, watercress, pepper, spring onions and cucumber and toss in the oil-free French dressing. Serve the salad with the lasagne.

Baconburgers with Pineapple and Green Beans
Serves 1: 330 calories

2 Birds Eye Baconburgers 225g (8 oz) slice melon *or*
2 rings pineapple canned 1 Kiwi fruit
in natural juice, drained
125g (4 oz) runner beans,
fresh *or* frozen

Grill the baconburgers thoroughly. Boil the runner beans. Place a pineapple ring on each baconburger. Return to the grill until hot. Serve with the beans. Follow with the melon or Kiwi fruit.

Meat Pudding and Vegetables
Serves 1: 335 calories

142-g (5-oz) can Goblins Meat Pudding
125g (4 oz) frozen runner beans
125g (4 oz) drained canned carrots

Cook the meat pudding and the runner beans as instructed. Heat the carrots and serve with the meat pudding and runner beans.

Smoked Haddock with Poached Egg
Serves 1: 335 calories

170-g (6-oz) packet Findus Buttered Smoked Haddock
1 egg, size 3
1 slice bread from a large, medium-sliced loaf

Cook the smoked haddock as instructed. Poach the egg in water or in a non-stick poacher. Place the fish on a plate with the poached egg on top. Serve with the unbuttered bread.

Chicken Crepes with Sweetcorn
Serves 1: 340 calories

214-g (8½-oz) Findus Chicken Crepes with Mushroom
  Sauce
125g (4 oz) sweetcorn, frozen or canned

Cook the crepes as instructed. Boil or heat the sweetcorn and serve with the crepes.

Scotch Egg and Salad
Serves 1: 345 calories

1 Walls Scotch Egg
mixed salad of tomato, lettuce, cucumber, cress,
   radishes and spring onions
15ml (1 tablespoon) Waistline or Heinz Low-Calorie
   Salad Cream

Serve the Scotch egg with the salad and salad cream.

Bacon Sandwich
Serves 1: 345 calories

2 rashers back bacon
2 slices bread from a large, medium-sliced loaf
15ml (1 tablespoon) tomato ketchup

Crisply grill the bacon and sandwich between the slices of
bread with the tomato ketchup.

Minced Beef with Rice
Serves 1: 350 calories

1 individual pack Ross Minced Beef and Vegetables
50g (2 oz) rice

Cook the minced beef as instructed. Boil the rice and serve
with the mince.

Pizza plus Banana
Serves 1: 350 calories

1 individual Birds Eye Tomato and Cheese Pizza
1 medium banana

Cook the pizza as instructed and follow with the banana.

Pizza with Baked Potato
Serves 1: 355 calories

150g (5 oz) potato
1 small St Michael Marguerita Pizza, 113g (4 oz)

Bake the potato in its jacket until soft when pinched. Cook the pizza as instructed and serve with the potato.

Braised Liver with Vegetables
Serves 1: 355 calories

1 pack Birds Eye Liver with Onion and Gravy
125g (4 oz) frozen mixed vegetables
1/2 medium packet Smash

Cook the liver and mixed vegetables as instructed. Make up the Smash and serve with the liver and vegetables.

Soup Meal plus Fruit
Serves 1: 360 calories

425-g (15-oz) can Campbells Main Course Steak &
    Kidney *or* Vegetable Soup
1 slice bread from a large, medium-sliced loaf
125g (4 oz) black grapes *or* 1 medium orange

Heat the soup and serve with the unbuttered bread.
Follow with the fruit.

Vegetable and Prawn Curry
Serves 1: 360 calories

1 packet Findus Vegetable   30ml (2 tablespoons)
    and Prawn Curry   natural yogurt
50g (2 oz) cucumber   salt and pepper

Cook the curry as instructed. Dice the cucumber, mix
with the yogurt and season. Serve with the curry.

Sausages and Beans
Serves 1: 375 calories

2 pork sausages
150-g (5.3-oz) can baked beans in tomato sauce
15ml (1 tablespoon) brown sauce

Grill the pork sausages well. Heat the baked beans and
serve with the sausages and sauce.

Shepherd's Pie with Baked Beans
Serves 1: 380 calories

1 Findus Shepherd's Pie, 227g (8 oz)
150-g (5.3-oz) can baked beans with tomato sauce

Cook the shepherd's pie as instructed. Heat the baked beans and serve with the pie.

Shepherd's Pie and Green Beans plus Banana
Serves 1: 390 calories

1 Findus Shepherd's Pie, 227g (8 oz)	15ml (1 level tablespoon) tomato ketchup *or* brown sauce
125g (4 oz) runner beans, fresh *or* frozen	1 small banana

Cook the shepherd's pie as instructed. Boil the beans and serve with the shepherd's pie and sauce. Follow with the banana.

Mackerel with Gooseberries
Serves 1: 385 calories

1 whole mackerel, 225g (8 oz)	30ml (2 tablespoons) water
50g (2 oz) gooseberries	5ml (1 level teaspoon) sugar
125g (4 oz) French or runner beans	

Clean and then grill the mackerel. While it is cooking place the gooseberries in a small saucepan with the water, cover and simmer until tender. Add the sugar and stir until dissolved. Boil the beans and serve with the mackerel and gooseberry sauce.

Savoury Pie and Salad
Serves 1: 395 calories

1 individual Kraft Cheese and Tomato Pie
lettuce, cucumber, cress, spring onions and green
 pepper
30ml (2 tablespoons) oil-free French dressing

Cook the pie as instructed. Make a green salad with the
lettuce, cucumber, cress, spring onions and green pepper
and toss in the dressing. Serve with the pie.

French Bread Pizza with Coleslaw
Serves 1: 395 calories

1 Findus French Bread Pizza, Italian Style Sausage
142-g (5-oz) carton St Ivel Coleslaw in Low-Calorie
 Dressing

Cook the pizza as instructed and serve with the coleslaw.

Chicken in Mushroom Sauce with Rice
Serves 1: 415 calories

205-g (7.23-oz) can Shippams Chunky Chicken in
 Mushroom Sauce
25g (1 oz) long-grain rice

Boil the rice. Heat the chicken and serve with the rice.

Quick Meals for Two

There may be times when you want to share a quick meal with your husband or a visiting friend. Perhaps the kids have gone off to a football match and you're too tired after doing the Saturday shopping to go to a lot of trouble. Or a dieting friend may suggest you share a low-calorie lunch rather than risk the temptations of local cafés or coffee bars.

All the following meals can be cooked quickly with little preparation. They can easily be kept in your freezer or store cupboard in case you unexpectedly need to hustle something up. And they are all very conveniently portion-controlled so you have little to weigh and measure.

If you wish, you can serve your husband or a non-dieting friend with extra vegetables or even a portion of oven or grill chips. We suggest you use these, rather than fry your own, because you can take just one portion out of the freezer and don't have the problem of 'disposing' of any leftover chips if you happen to cut too big a potato! If you've got sneaky fingers, though, best tell the chip-eater to give them a smack if they stray into the vicinity of his or her plate!

Pilchard Salad
Serves 2: 230 calories per portion

227-g (8-oz) can Princes
   Pilchards in Tomato
   Sauce
1 egg, size 3
3 tomatoes
2 spring onions

50g (2 oz) cucumber
lettuce
30ml (2 tablespoons)
   Heinz *or* Waistline
   Low-Calorie Salad
   Cream

Hardboil the egg. Cool and quarter. Quarter the tomatoes. Discard roots and tough green leaves of spring onions. Slice cucumber. Divide pilchards between two plates and arrange egg and salad around them. Serve with low-calorie salad cream.

Cheese and Ham Pancakes with Tomatoes
Serves 2: 250 calories per portion

4 Birds Eye Cheese and Ham Savoury Pancakes
4 tomatoes
30ml (2 tablespoons) brown sauce

Bake the pancakes without any added fat at 190°C (375°F), gas mark 5, for 15 minutes. Halve tomatoes and bake alongside the pancakes for the last 5 minutes. Serve with brown sauce.

Macaroni Cheese and Green Salad
Serves 2: 250 calories per portion

1 pack Rossi Macaroni Cheese
lettuce, cucumber, green pepper and cress
45ml (3 tablespoons) oil-free French dressing

Cook the macaroni cheese as instructed. Make up a green salad from the lettuce, cucumber, green pepper and cress and toss in the oil-free French dressing. Serve with the macaroni cheese.

Haddock Savoury and Peas
Serves 2: 260 calories per portion

1 pack Marco and Carlo Golden Haddock Savoury
125g (4 oz) frozen peas

Cook the haddock savoury as instructed. Boil the peas and serve with the fish.

Ham and Mushroom Pizza with Tomatoes
Serves 2: 265 calories per portion

1 7-inch Ross Ham and Mushroom Pizza
4 tomatoes
1.25ml (1/4 level teaspoon) dried basil

Cook the pizza as instructed. Halve the tomatoes and sprinkle with basil. Bake alongside the pizza for the last 5 minutes.

Chicklets and Savoury Mash
Serves 2: 265 calories per portion

2 Birds Eye Chicklets
1 packet Yeoman Savoury Mash with Bacon Flavoured
  Pieces
225g (8 oz) frozen French beans *or* haricots verts

Grill the chicklets without any added fat. Make up the
mash as instructed. Boil the beans and serve with the
chicklets and mash.

Cannelloni and Tomato Salad
Serves 2: 275 calories per portion

1 pack Birds Eye	2 spring onions
Cannelloni	30ml (2 tablespoons)
3 tomatoes	oil-free French dressing

Cook the cannelloni as instructed. Slice the tomatoes.
Discard roots and tough green leaves of spring onions and
finely slice bulbs. Toss tomatoes and onion in oil-free
French dressing and serve with cannelloni.

Fish Pie and Vegetables
Serves 2: 290 calories per portion

1 Birds Eye Captain's Pie
225g (8 oz) frozen runner beans
225g (8 oz) fresh or frozen carrots

Cook the Captain's Pie as instructed. Boil the vegetables
and serve with the pie.

Onion Soup plus Paella
Serves 2: 290 calories per portion

298-g (10½-oz) can Campbell's Condensed Onion Soup
1 pack Birds Eye Paella

Make up the soup as instructed. Cook the paella as instructed and eat after the soup.

Fish Casserole and Vegetables
Serves 2: 295 calories per portion

1 pack St Michael Fish Casserole
225g (8 oz) frozen runner beans
225g (8 oz) drained canned new potatoes

Cook the fish casserole as instructed. Boil the beans, heat the potatoes and serve with the casserole.

Speedy Ham Risotto
Serves 2: 295 calories per portion

227-g (8-oz) packet Birds Eye Rice, Sweetcorn and
    Peppers
113-g (4-oz) lean cooked ham
30ml (2 level tablespoons) Parmesan cheese

Cook the vegetable rice as instructed. Discard all visible fat from ham and chop the lean. Stir into the hot rice and sprinkle Parmesan cheese on top.

Lasagne and Salad
Serves 2: 305 calories per portion

1 British Home Stores Lasagne
198-g (7-oz) carton St Ivel Crispy Vegetable Salad in
   Vinaigrette

Cook the lasagne as instructed and serve with the salad.

Bacon Fingers and Chips
Serves 2: 315 calories per portion

4 Danish Prime Bacon Fingers
225g (8-oz) Findus Grill Chips
30ml (2 tablespoons) tomato ketchup *or* brown sauce

Grill the bacon fingers as instructed without added fat.
Grill the chips as instructed and serve with bacon fingers
and sauce.

Battered Cod and Mushy Peas
Serves 2: 315 calories per portion

2 Birds Eye Oven Crispy   vinegar
   Cod Steaks   30ml (2 tablespoons)
304-g (10.7-oz) can   tomato ketchup
   Batchelor's Mushy Peas

Bake the cod steaks as instructed. Heat the mushy peas
and serve with the fish, a little vinegar and tomato
ketchup.

Double Decker and Baked Beans
Serves 2: 330 calories per portion

2 Findus Beef Double Deckers
450-g (15.9-oz) can baked beans in tomato sauce

Bake the Double Deckers as instructed, heat baked beans and serve.

Meatballs with Mash and Carrots
Serves 2: 330 calories

425-g (15-oz) can Campbell's Beef Meatballs and Gravy
225g (8 oz) drained canned carrots
1 medium packet Smash

Heat the meatballs and carrots in a small saucepan. Make up the Smash as instructed and serve with the meatballs and carrots.

Prawn Curry
Serves 2: 335 calories per portion

1 2-portion pack Vesta Prawn Curry
30ml (2 level tablespoons) Sherwoods Tomato and Chilli
  Chutney

Make up the prawn curry as instructed and serve with the chutney.

Vegetable Pizza with Coleslaw
Serves 2: 360 calories per portion

1 Birds Eye Special Vegetable Pizza, 284g (10 oz)
227-g (8-oz) carton Eden Vale Coleslaw in Vinaigrette

Cook the pizza as instructed and serve with the cole-slaw.

Beef Biriani with Cucumber Salad
Serves 2: 370 calories per portion

1 2-portion pack Vesta Beef Biriani	60ml (4 level tablespoons) natural yogurt
125g (4 oz) cucumber	salt and pepper

Cook the Beef Biriani as instructed but without adding fat. Dice the cucumber and mix with the yogurt. Season with salt and pepper and serve with the beef.

Cottage Pie and Green Beans
Serves 2: 380 calories per portion

1 Kraft Cheesy Topped Cottage Pie, 454g (16 oz)
225g (8 oz) green runner beans

Cook the cottage pie as instructed. Boil the beans and serve with the pie.

Egg, Cheese and Bacon Flan with Green Salad
Serves 2: 390 calories per portion

1 Findus Egg, Cheese and Bacon Flan
lettuce, cucumber, cress and spring onions
45ml (3 tablespoons) oil-free French dressing

Cook the flan as instructed. Make a green salad with the
lettuce, cucumber, cress and spring onions and toss in the
oil-free French dressing. Serve with the flan.

Beef and Kidney Stew with Mash
Serves 2: 390 calories per portion

417-g (14.7-oz) can Batchelor's Beef and Kidney
223-g (7.9-oz) can Batchelor's Butter Beans
1 medium packet Smash

Empty the beef and kidney into a small saucepan. Drain
the butter beans, add to the pan and heat through gently.
Make up the Smash as instructed and serve with the
stew.

Faggots with Processed Peas
Serves 2: 460 calories per portion

1 pack Birds Eye Faggots in Sauce, 369g (13 oz)
283-g (10-oz) can processed peas

Cook the faggots as instructed. Heat the peas, drain and
serve with the faggots.

Meals to Eat with the Family

An excuse often put forward by failed slimmers is that it is impossible to diet while feeding the family. So in this chapter we give some low-calorie recipes that you can share with others. No, we're not suggesting that you put the family on a diet (unless, of course, they are over-weight). With a serving of vegetables, these recipes should satisfy most appetites. Let your family choose whatever vegetables they would normally eat, and keep your own vegetables calorie-counted. To help you do this we have devised an easy way for you to measure out portions from the family pot (see page 133).

All recipes serve four. If there are only two in your family, many recipes can be made in half the quantity or you could freeze extra casserole portions for another day. If you are a family of three, take out your quarter portion and make sure the extra amount is divided between non-dieting members or frozen. Calories range from 135 to 400 per portion and there are meals suitable for brunch, lunch and dinner.

We have split this chapter into chicken, beef, pork, ham, liver and kidney, sausage, fish and vegetarian meals. It is easy, therefore, to choose meals your family will like, while also keeping an eye on your weekly budget.

If you have had a weight problem since you were a child, it could well be that some of the eating habits you learned from your mother made you fat. While you are getting yourself slim, you could be helping your family learn some very good eating habits – ones that will keep them healthy, too.

CHICKEN MEALS

Chinese Chicken and Tongue Salad
Serves 4: 165 calories per portion

175g (6 oz) cooked
    chicken
75g (3 oz) tongue
3 sticks celery
2 eating apples
225g (8 oz) bean sprouts

60ml (4 tablespoons)
    oil-free French dressing
5ml (1 teaspoon) Soy
    sauce
salt and pepper

Discard any skin from the chicken. Cut the chicken and tongue into bite-size pieces. Roughly chop the celery. Core and dice the apples but leave the skin on. Mix together chicken, tongue, celery, apple and bean sprouts. Add oil-free French dressing and Soy sauce and toss gently. Season with salt and pepper and serve.

Chicken in Pepper and Tomato Sauce
Serves 4: 200 calories per portion

575g (1¼ lb) boned
  chicken breast fillets
1 medium onion
225g (8 oz) tomatoes
1 green pepper
150ml (¼ pint) boiling
  water

½ chicken stock cube
1 bay leaf
2.5ml (½ level) teaspoon
  dried basil
salt and pepper
15ml (1 level tablespoon)
  cornflour

Discard the skin from the chicken breasts. Chop the onion. Peel and quarter the tomatoes. Discard white pith and seeds from pepper and cut flesh into strips. Dissolve stock cube in boiling water. Place the chicken, onion, tomatoes, pepper, stock, bay leaf and basil in a saucepan, and season with salt and pepper. Cover the pan and simmer gently for 40 minutes. Blend the cornflour with a little cold water until smooth and then add to the pan, stirring all the time. Simmer for 1–2 minutes.

Tandoori Chicken
Serves 4: 205 calories per portion

4 chicken breasts, 175g (6
  oz) each
20ml (4 level teaspoons)
  Sharwood's Tandoori
  Curry Powder
pinch salt

60ml (4 tablespoons)
  natural yogurt
20ml (4 teaspoons) lemon
  juice
2 medium bananas
little lemon juice

Skin the chicken breasts and make four deep cuts in the flesh of each. Place in a shallow, non-metal dish. Mix together the Tandoori Curry Powder, yogurt, lemon juice and salt, then spread over the chicken breasts. Cover with clear food wrap and refrigerate for at least 8 hours (24 hours is even better if you have time). Turn over once or twice while marinading.

When ready, preheat a moderate grill and grill the chicken for 10 minutes on each side. Thickly slice the bananas, toss in the lemon juice and serve with the chicken.

Chicken in Asparagus Sauce
Serves 4: 215 calories per portion

450g (1 lb) skinless chicken breast fillets
175g (6 oz) button mushrooms
50g (2 oz) lean cooked ham

295-g (10.4-oz) can condensed asparagus soup
30ml (2 tablespoons) skimmed milk

Place the chicken breast fillets in a shallow wide-based saucepan. Quarter the mushrooms if large, but leave whole if small. Discard all visible fat from the ham and cut the lean into squares. Add mushrooms, ham, undiluted soup and skimmed milk to the chicken and bring to the boil. Stir well, cover the pan and simmer for 25 minutes. Serve hot.

Chicken in Grape Sauce
Serves 4: 225 calories per portion

4 chicken breasts, 175g
  (6 oz) each
1 chicken stock cube
425ml (³/₄ pint) boiling
  water
pinch dried tarragon *or*
  mixed herbs

225g (8 oz) white grapes
30ml (2 level tablespoons)
  cornflour
25g (1 oz) powdered
  skimmed milk
salt and pepper

Skin the chicken breasts and place in a saucepan. Dissolve the stock cube in the boiling water and pour over the chicken. Sprinkle on the tarragon or mixed herbs and season with salt and pepper. Cover the pan and simmer gently for 30 minutes. Halve and pip the grapes. Drain the chicken and reserve stock. If necessary add a little extra cold water to stock to make up to 300ml (12 fl oz). Keep the breasts warm. Blend the cornflour and powdered skimmed milk with a little of the reserved stock and then return to the pan with the remaining stock. Bring to the boil, stirring continuously and simmer for 2 minutes. Add the grapes and heat through. Pour over the chicken and serve.

Chicken and Pineapple Casserole
Serves 4: 255 calories per portion

4 chicken leg joints, 227g (8 oz) each
376-g (13¼-oz) can pineapple in natural juice
1 medium onion
10ml (2 teaspoons) Soy sauce

1 green pepper
1 chicken stock cube
275ml (½ pint) boiling water
salt and pepper
30ml (2 level tablespoons) cornflour

Skin the chicken joints and place in a casserole with the pineapple and its juice. Chop the onion. Discard pith and seeds from the pepper and dice flesh. Add to casserole with onion, Soy sauce, and stock cube dissolved in boiling water. Season, cover dish and cook at 190°C (375°F), gas mark 5, for about 45 minutes. Blend cornflour with a little cold water and stir into casserole. Cook for 15 minutes longer.

Chicken Paprika
Serves 4: 265 calories per portion

4 chicken leg joints, 250g (9 oz) each
30ml (2 level tablespoons) paprika
30ml (2 level tablespoons) flour
1 large onion
425ml (¾ pint) tomato juice

1 green pepper
150ml (¼ pint) water
5ml (1 level teaspoon) sugar
5ml (1 level teaspoon) salt
1 bay leaf
1 small carton natural yogurt

Skin the chicken joints, then toss in the paprika and flour. Place in a casserole dish. Chop the onion. Discard the pith and seeds from the pepper and slice the flesh. Add the onion and pepper to the casserole with the tomato juice, water, sugar, salt and bay leaf. Cover the dish and cook at 180°C (350°F), gas mark 4 for 1 hour. Stir in the yogurt and cook for 5 minutes more.

Chicken, Ham and Rice Salad
Serves 4: 275 calories per portion

125g (4 oz) long-grain rice	198-g (7-oz) can sweetcorn
90ml (6 tablespoons) oil-free French dressing	227-g (8-oz) can pineapple in natural juice
125g (4 oz) cooked chicken	175g (6-oz) cucumber
125g (4 oz) lean cooked ham	1 small red *or* green pepper
	salt and pepper

Cook long-grain rice as instructed on the packet. Drain into a sieve, rinse under the cold tap and then drain again. Put in a bowl and mix well with oil-free French dressing. Discard any skin from the chicken and fat from the ham. Cut the meats into small pieces. Drain sweetcorn and pineapple and cut the pineapple into cubes. Dice the cucumber. Discard white pith and seeds from the pepper and dice the flesh. Mix all the ingredients together and season with salt and pepper. Cover with clear food wrap and chill for half an hour before serving.

Curried Chicken and Banana Salad
Serves 4: 325 calories per portion

450g (1 lb) cooked chicken
2 small cartons natural
  yogurt
60ml (4 tablespoons)
  mango chutney
5ml (1 level teaspoon)
  curry paste or powder
salt and pepper

1 green pepper
175g (6 oz) cucumber
2 medium bananas
30ml (2 tablespoons)
  lemon juice
45ml (3 level tablespoons)
  raisins

Discard any skin from the chicken and cut the flesh into
bite-size pieces. Mix together the yogurt, mango chutney
and curry paste or powder. Season with salt and pepper.
Discard pith and seeds from pepper and dice flesh. Dice
cucumber. Peel and thickly slice bananas and toss in
lemon juice. Add chicken, pepper, cucumber, bananas
and raisins to curry dressing and mix well.

BEEF MEALS

Beef Coleslaw in Mustard Dressing
Serves 4: 135 calories per portion

225g (8 oz) lean roast
  topside of beef
225g (8 oz) white cabbage
1 small red *or* green
  pepper
3 spring onions

1 individual carton natural
  yogurt
15ml (1 level tablespoon)
  Colman's Mustard with
  Horseradish
salt and pepper

Discard all visible fat from the beef and cut the lean into
small strips. Shred the cabbage. Discard white pith and

seeds from the pepper and dice the flesh. Discard the tough green stems from spring onions and thinly slice the white. Mix yogurt with the mustard and season with salt and pepper. Stir in the beef and vegetables, cover with clear food wrap and chill.

Carbonnade of Beef
Serves 4: 185 calories per portion

450g (1 lb) lean braising
   steak
1 medium onion
1 clove garlic
283-ml (1/2-pint) can
   brown ale
1/2 beef stock cube

5ml (1 level teaspoon)
   brown sugar
5ml (1 teaspoon) vinegar
1 bay leaf
salt and pepper
20ml (4 level teaspoons)
   cornflour

Discard any visible fat from the braising steak and cut the lean into squares. Chop the onion and crush the garlic. Place in a casserole dish with the beef. Pour over the brown ale. Crumble the stock cube and add to casserole with brown sugar, vinegar and bay leaf. Cover the dish and cook at 150°C (300°F), gas mark 2 for 2 hours. Blend cornflour with a little cold water until smooth, then stir into the casserole. Return to the oven for a further hour.

Steak and Prune Casserole
Serves 4: 210 calories per portion

450g (1 lb) lean braising
  steak
125g (4 oz) dried prunes
1 medium onion
5ml (1 teaspoon) Soy
  Sauce
15ml (1 tablespoon) brown
  sauce

5ml (1 teaspoon) vinegar
5ml (1 level teaspoon)
  brown sugar
5ml (1 level teaspoon) salt
275ml (½ pint) water
pepper
15ml (1 level tablespoon)
  cornflour

Discard all visible fat from the meat and cut the lean into cubes. Place in a casserole with the prunes. Chop the onion and add to the casserole. Mix together the soy sauce, brown sauce, vinegar, brown sugar, salt and water and pour over the meat and prunes. Season with pepper, cover the dish and cook at 170° (325°F), gas mark 3, for 2 hours or until the meat is tender. Blend the cornflour with a little cold water until smooth. Add to the casserole and cook for another ½ hour.

Steak, Kidney and Mushroom Casserole
Serves 4: 225 calories per portion

450g (1 lb) braising steak
225g (8 oz) lamb's *or* pig's
  kidneys
225g (8 oz) mushrooms
1 onion
275ml (½ pint) water
1 beef stock cube

15ml (1 tablespoon)
  Worcestershire sauce
15ml (1 level tablespoon)
  tomato purée
salt and pepper
15ml (1 level tablespoon)
  cornflour

Discard fat from braising steak and cut into cubes. Halve and core the kidneys and cut into small pieces. If the mushrooms are large, cut into four. If they are small, leave whole. Chop the onion. Place the stewing steak, kidney, mushrooms and onion in a casserole dish. Add the water, stock cube, Worcestershire sauce and tomato purée and season with salt and pepper. Cover the dish and cook at 170°C (325°F), gas mark 3, for 2 hours. Blend the cornflour with a little cold water, add to the casserole and cook for another ½ hour.

Beef and Butter Bean Casserole
Serves 4: 250 calories per portion

450g (1 lb) lean stewing
  steak
30ml (2 level tablespoons)
  plain flour
2 medium carrots
2 sticks celery
1 medium onion
30ml (2 level tablespoons)
  tomato purée

1 beef stock cube
425ml (¾ pint) boiling
  water
salt and pepper
425-g (15-oz) can butter
  beans

Discard all visible fat from the beef and cut the lean into cubes. Toss in the flour and place in a casserole dish with any excess flour. Slice the carrots and celery. Chop the onion. Add the vegetables to the casserole. Dissolve the tomato purée and stock cube in the boiling water and pour over the meat and vegetables. Season with salt and pepper, cover the dish and cook in the oven at 170°C (325°F), gas mark 3, for 2 hours. Drain the butter beans, add to the casserole and cook for another 15 minutes.

Moussaka
Serves 4: 290 calories per portion

1 large aubergine	¹/₂ beef stock cube
salt and pepper	150ml (¹/₄ pint) boiling
450g (1 lb) minced beef	water
15ml (1 level tablespoon)	2 tomatoes
flour	individual carton natural
1 clove garlic	yogurt
1 medium onion	1 egg, size 3
5ml (1 level teaspoon)	25g (1 oz) grated Cheddar
mixed dried herbs	cheese
30ml (2 level tablespoons)	pinch ground nutmeg.
tomato purée	

Slice the aubergine and arrange on a plate. Sprinkle with salt and leave to stand for 30 minutes. Drain away any liquid that comes out of the slices. Bring a large pan of water to the boil, add the aubergine and simmer for just 1 minute. Drain in a colander, then pat dry with kitchen paper. Brown the minced beef in a non-stick frying pan until the fat runs out. Drain away the fat and place the mince in a saucepan. Stir in the flour. Crush the garlic and finely chop the onion. Add to mince with mixed dried herbs and tomato purée. Dissolve the stock cube in the boiling water and add to the pan. Season. Stir well, then cover the pan and simmer gently for about 25 minutes. Spread half the mince in an ovenproof dish, then cover with the aubergine slices. Slice the tomatoes and arrange on top. Cover with the remaining mince. Whisk together the yogurt, egg, grated Cheddar and nutmeg. Season with salt and pepper and pour over the mince. Bake at 180°C (350°F), gas mark 4, for 25 minutes.

Chilli con Carne
Serves 4: 295 calories per portion

450g (1 lb) minced beef
1 medium onion
397-g (14-oz) can tomatoes
5ml (1 level teaspoon)
  chilli powder
10ml (2 level teaspoons)
  brown sugar

1 beef stock cube
salt and pepper
10ml (2 level teaspoons)
  cornflour
425-g (15-oz) can red
  kidney beans

Brown the minced beef in a non-stick frying pan until the fat runs out. Drain off the fat and place the mince in a saucepan. Chop the onion and add to the pan with the tomatoes, stock cube, chilli powder and sugar. Season with salt and pepper. Cover the pan and simmer gently for 30 minutes. Blend the cornflour with a little cold water until smooth. Add to the pan, stirring all the time and simmer for 2 minutes. Drain the beans. Add to the pan and heat through gently.

Herby Beef Cobbler
Serves 4: 355 calories per portion

450g (1 lb) minced beef
15ml (1 level tablespoon)
  flour
1 medium onion
227-g (8-oz) can tomatoes
150ml (¼ pint) water
1 beef stock cube
salt and pepper
125g (4 oz) self-raising
  flour

2.5ml (½ level teaspoon)
  baking powder
2.5ml (½ level teaspoon)
  dry mustard powder
2.5ml (½ level teaspoon)
  mixed dried herbs
25g (1 oz) butter *or*
  margarine
60–90ml (4–6 tablespoons)
  skimmed milk

Brown mince in a non-stick frying pan until the fat runs out. Drain off the fat and stir flour into the mince. Turn into a casserole dish. Finely chop the onion and add to mince with tomatoes, water and crumbled stock cube. Stir to mix and season with salt and pepper. Cover the dish and cook in the oven at 190°C (375°F), gas mark 5 for 40 minutes. Sieve together self-raising flour, baking powder, dry mustard and 2.5ml (½ level teaspoon) salt. Add herbs and rub in butter or margarine. Add enough milk to make a soft dough and then roll out on a lightly floured board to a ¼-inch thickness. Cut into 1-inch rounds and arrange on top of the mince. Return to the oven and cook, uncovered, for another 20 minutes.

Savoury Mince with Rice
Serves 4: 365 calories per portion

450g (1 lb) minced beef	5ml (1 teaspoon)
1 medium onion	Worcestershire sauce
½ green pepper	salt and pepper
50g (2 oz) mushrooms	425ml (¾ pint) water
2 sticks celery	1 beef stock cube
397-g (14-oz) can tomatoes	175g (6 oz) long-grain rice

Brown the mince in a non-stick frying pan until all the fat runs out. Drain off and discard the fat. Place mince in a saucepan. Chop the onion. Discard pith and seeds from pepper and dice flesh. Chop mushrooms and celery. Add all vegetables to mince with tomatoes and their juice and Worcestershire sauce. Season with salt and pepper. Bring to the boil, cover the pan and simmer gently for 30 minutes. While the mince is cooking, place the water and stock cube in another pan. Bring to the boil and stir to dissolve the stock cube. Add the rice and bring back to the boil, stirring all the time. Cover the pan and simmer gently for 20 minutes or until the stock is absorbed and the rice is just tender. Check frequently and add a little more water if the rice gets too dry and starts to stick. Add the rice to the mince, cover the pan and simmer for another 10–15 minutes. Serve hot.

Shepherd's Pie
Serves 4: 375 calories per portion

450g (1 lb) minced beef
30ml (2 level tablespoons) flour
1 medium onion
15ml (1 level tablespoon) tomato purée
2.5ml (½ level teaspoon) mixed dried herbs
½ beef stock cube
175ml (6 fl. oz) boiling water
salt and pepper
675g (1½ lb) potatoes, peeled
15g (½ oz) low-fat spread
60ml (4 tablespoons) skimmed milk

Brown the mince in a non-stick pan until the fat runs out. Discard the fat. Stir the flour into the mince. Chop the onion and add to mince, with tomato purée and herbs. Turn into an ovenproof dish. Dissolve stock cube in the water, then stir into the meat mixture. Season with salt and pepper. Cover the dish and cook in the oven at 180°C (350°F), gas mark 4, for 40 minutes. While meat is cooking, boil the potatoes and mash with the low-fat spread and milk. Season with salt and pepper. Spread mashed potato over the mince mixture. Turn the oven up to 200°C (400°F), gas mark 6, and cook for a further 20 minutes.

Spaghetti Bolognese
Serves 4: 375 calories per portion

350g (12 oz) minced beef	1 carrot
30ml (2 level tablespoons) flour	397-g (14-oz) can tomatoes
125g (4 oz) chicken livers	2.5ml (½ level teaspoon) mixed dried herbs
1 medium onion	275ml (½ pint) water
1 clove garlic	1 beef stock cube
125g (4 oz) mushrooms	salt and pepper
1 stick celery	175g (6 oz) spaghetti

Brown the mince in a non-stick frying pan, then discard the fat that runs out. Put the mince into a saucepan and stir in flour. Trim chicken livers and cut into small pieces. Finely chop the onion and crush the garlic. Chop the mushrooms. Cut the celery and carrot into small dice. Add chicken livers and vegetables to the mince with tomatoes and their juice, herbs, water and crumbled stock cube. Season with salt and pepper. Bring to the boil, stir well, cover the pan and simmer gently for 1 hour. Add a little more water if necessary during cooking. Boil the spaghetti as instructed on the packet. Drain, divide between four plates and serve the sauce on top.

Note If you want to add Parmesan cheese allow an extra 30 calories per 15ml (1 level tablespoon).

Corned Beef and Baked Bean Pie
Serves 4: 395 calories per portion

340-g (12-oz) can corned
  beef
397-g (14-oz) can sliced
  carrots
450-g (15.9-oz) can baked
  beans in tomato sauce

30ml (2 tablespoons)
  bottled brown sauce
salt and pepper
1 large packet Cadbury's
  Smash

Cut the corned beef into cubes. Drain the carrots and mix gently with corned beef, beans, brown sauce and seasoning. Turn into an ovenproof dish. Make up the Smash as instructed and spread over the meat and bean mixture. Bake at 200°C (400°F), gas mark 6, for 20–25 minutes or until the potato is lightly browned and the dish is hot right through.

Curried Beef Pancakes
Serves 4: 400 calories per portion
Pancakes:
 125g (4 oz) plain flour
pinch salt
1 egg, size 3

275ml (½ pint) skimmed
  milk
2.5ml (½ teaspoon) oil

Sauce:
 30ml (2 level tablespoons)
  cornflour
5ml (1 level teaspoon)
  curry powder
60ml (4 level tablespoons)
  powdered skimmed
  milk

575ml (1 pint) water
30ml (2 level tablespoons)
  apricot jam
60ml (4 level tablespoons)
  mango chutney
1 beef stock cube

Filling:

350g (12 oz) minced beef	30ml (2 level tablespoons)
1 medium onion	tomato paste
5ml (1 level teaspoon)	salt and pepper
curry powder	

Pancakes Place the flour, salt, egg and skimmed milk in a blender and blend until smooth. Grease a small non-stick frying pan with some of the oil (use remainder as necessary) and cook 12 pancakes. Stack and set aside.

Sauce Mix the cornflour, curry powder, powdered skimmed milk and a little of the water to make a smooth paste. Stir in the remaining water and pour into a saucepan. Add apricot jam, mango chutney and crumbled stock cube and bring to the boil, stirring all the time. Simmer for 2 minutes and set aside.

Filling Brown the minced beef in a non-stick frying pan and drain off all the fat. Turn the mince into a small saucepan. Finely chop the onion and add to the mince with the curry powder, tomato paste and one third of the prepared sauce. Season with salt and pepper. Cover the pan and simmer for 15–20 minutes, stirring occasionally and adding a little more water if necessary. Divide the filling between the pancakes and roll up. Arrange in a single layer in an ovenproof dish, cover with foil and heat in the oven at 190°C (375°F), gas mark 5, for 10–15 minutes. Reheat the remaining sauce in a saucepan and serve with the pancakes.

PORK MEALS

Barbecued Pork Fillet
Serves 4: 230 calories per portion

450g (1 lb) pork
  tenderloin *or* fillet
15ml (1 tablespoon) Soy
  sauce
10ml (2 teaspoons)
  Worcestershire sauce
30ml (2 tablespoons)
  tomato ketchup
15ml (1 tablespoon)
  bottled brown sauce

10ml (2 level teaspoons)
  honey
2.5ml (½ level teaspoon)
  French mustard
1 medium onion
15g (½ oz) butter *or*
  margarine
150ml (¼ pint) boiling
  water
½ chicken stock cube

Discard any fat from the pork tenderloin or fillet and cut the lean into bite-size pieces. Mix together the Soy sauce, Worcestershire sauce, tomato ketchup, brown sauce, honey and mustard, then add the pork. Stir well so that all the pieces of pork are coated. Cover the dish and leave in the refrigerator to marinate for 2-8 hours. Finely chop the onion. Melt the butter or margarine in a large frying pan and cook the onion over a moderate heat until soft. Drain the pork from the marinade and add to the pan. Cook for a few minutes, turning once, until it changes colour. Transfer the onion and pork to a saucepan and add the marinade. Dissolve the stock cube in the water and add to the pan. Cover the pan and simmer pork gently for 30–40 minutes or until tender. Remove the pork to a serving dish and keep warm. Boil the pan rapidly without a lid on, stirring frequently until the sauce is sticky and reduced by half. Pour over the pork and serve.

Fruity Pork Casserole
Serves 4: 270 calories per portion

450g (1 lb) lean, boneless
   leg of pork
1 small onion
175g (6 oz) carrots
8 dried apricots
grated rind and juice of 1
   orange
1 chicken stock cube

275ml (½ pint) boiling
   water
5ml (1 teaspoon) Soy
   Sauce
salt and pepper
20ml (4 level teaspoons)
   cornflour

Discard all visible fat from the pork, then cut the lean into
bite-size pieces. Chop the onion and slice carrots. Place
the pork, onion, carrots and dried apricots in a casserole
dish. Add the finely grated rind and juice of the orange.
Dissolve the stock cube in boiling water, then stir in Soy
sauce. Pour over meat in the casserole dish and season
with salt and pepper. Cover the dish and cook at 180°C
(350°F), gas mark 4, for 45 minutes. Blend cornflour with
a little cold water and stir into the casserole. Return to the
oven and cook for a further 30 minutes.

LIVER AND KIDNEY MEALS

Liver and Orange Casserole
Serves 4: 245 calories per portion

450g (1 lb) lamb's liver
15ml (1 level tablespoon)
   plain flour
salt and pepper
1.25ml (¼ level teaspoon)
   dried thyme
1 medium orange

1 medium onion
125g (4 oz) carrots
15ml (1 level tablespoon)
   tomato purée
1 beef stock cube
275ml (½ pint) boiling
   water

Slice the liver, then rinse under cold water. Pat dry with kitchen paper. Season flour with salt and pepper, then toss the liver in it. Place liver in a casserole and sprinkle on the thyme. Grate rind from half the orange and squeeze the juice from all of it. Chop the onion and thinly slice carrots. Add the orange rind and juice, onion and carrots to the casserole. Dissolve tomato purée and stock cube in boiling water and pour over the liver and vegetables. Season with salt and pepper. Cover the casserole and cook at 180°C (350°F), gas mark 4, for 1 hour.

Liver and Bacon Casserole
Serves 4: 265 calories per portion

450g (1 lb) lamb's *or* pig's liver

1 bacon picnic steak, 100g (3½ oz)

227-g (8-oz) can tomatoes

125g (4 oz) carrots

1 medium onion

1 beef stock cube

150ml (¼ pint) boiling water

5ml (1 level teaspoon) dried basil *or* mixed dried herbs

salt and pepper

15ml (1 level tablespoon) cornflour

Wash the liver under cold water, then pat dry with kitchen paper. Cut liver into small thick slices and place in a casserole dish. Cut the bacon steak into cubes and scatter over the liver. Drain the tomatoes and add the juice to the casserole. Roughly chop the tomatoes. Slice the carrots thinly and chop the onion. Add tomatoes, carrots and onions to the casserole. Dissolve the stock cube in water and pour over. Sprinkle on the herbs and season with salt and pepper. Cover the dish and cook at 190°C (375°F), gas mark 5, for 45 minutes. Blend the cornflour with a little cold water until smooth and stir into the casserole. Return to the oven and cook for a further 15 minutes.

Chicken Liver Pâté with Toast
Serves 4: 290 calories per portion

225g (8 oz) chicken livers
25g (1 oz) onion
60ml (4 tablespoons)
  chicken stock
5ml (1 level teaspoon)
  tomato purée

good pinch of mixed herbs
113-g (4-oz) carton curd *or*
  cottage cheese
salt and pepper
8 slices bread from a large,
  medium-sliced loaf

Roughly chop the chicken livers and finely chop the onion. Place in a small saucepan with stock, herbs and tomato purée. Cover the pan and simmer gently for 5 minutes. Leave to cool. Drain off any excess liquid and place the livers in a bowl with curd or cottage cheese. Mash with a fork until smooth. Toast the bread and serve with the pâté.

Note The rest of the family can have butter or margarine on their toast if they wish.

Liver and Prune Casserole
Serves 4: 300 calories per portion

125g (4 oz) prunes
2 medium onions
450g (1 lb) lamb's *or* pig's
  liver
2.5ml (½ level teaspoon)
  dried mixed herbs

salt and pepper
30ml (2 level tablespoons)
  cornflour
25g (1 oz) powdered
  skimmed milk

Soak the prunes overnight in cold water. Drain and place in a small pan with 275ml (½ pint) fresh water. Cover and simmer for 10 minutes. Drain and reserve the liquid. Slice the onions and place in a casserole dish with the liver and the prune liquid. Add the herbs and season with salt and pepper. Cover and cook in the oven at 180°C (350°F), gas mark 4, for 1½ hours. Blend the cornflour with the powdered skimmed milk and an extra 150ml (¼ pint) water. Add to the casserole with the prunes and cook for another 20 minutes.

Kidney Risotto
Serves 4: 320 calories per portion

450g (1 lb) lamb's kidneys
1 medium onion
15ml (1 tablespoon) oil
175g (6 oz) long-grain rice
125g (4 oz) mushrooms
1 beef stock cube
275ml (½ pint) boiling
  water

2.5ml (½ level teaspoon)
  mixed dried herbs
227-g (8-oz) can tomatoes
125g (4 oz) frozen mixed
  vegetables
salt and pepper

Halve and core the kidneys, then cut into pieces. Chop the onion, then cook in the oil in a large saucepan until soft. Add the rice and cook, stirring, for a minute. Slice the mushrooms. Dissolve the stock cube in boiling water and add to the pan with mushrooms, herbs and tomatoes plus juices. Season; bring to the boil and stir well. Cover the pan and simmer very gently for 15 minutes. Add the mixed vegetables, cover the pan again and cook for another 5–10 minutes. At the end of cooking the rice should be tender and the liquid should all be absorbed. If the mixture gets too dry during cooking and the rice starts to stick, add a little more boiling water.

Spaghetti with Chicken Liver Sauce
Serves 4: 375 calories per portion

450g (1 lb) chicken livers
50g (2 oz) lean cooked
  ham
225g (8 oz) button
  mushrooms
1 medium onion
60ml (4 level tablespoons)
  tomato purée

2.5ml (½ level teaspoon)
  mixed dried herbs
275ml (½ pint) water
1 chicken stock cube
salt and pepper
15ml (1 level tablespoon)
  cornflour
175g (6 oz) spaghetti

Trim the chicken livers and cut into small pieces. Discard fat from the ham and chop the lean. Thinly slice the mushrooms and finely chop onion. Place chicken livers, ham, mushrooms, onion, tomato purée, herbs, water and stock cube in a saucepan and season with salt and pepper. Bring to the boil, cover the pan and simmer gently for 15 minutes. Blend cornflour with a little cold water until smooth, then add to the pan, stirring all the time. Simmer for 1–2 minutes. While the sauce is cooking, boil the spaghetti in boiling, salted water for 10–12 minutes. Drain and serve the chicken liver sauce on top.

SAUSAGE MEALS

Sausage, Bean and Egg Toast
Serves 4: 245 calories per portion

2 pork chipolata sausages
2 eggs, size 3
450-g (15.9-oz) can baked
  beans in tomato sauce

30ml (2 tablespoons)
  tomato ketchup
4 slices bread from a large,
  medium-sliced loaf

Grill the pork chipolata sausages thoroughly. Hardboil the eggs. Cool in cold water, then shell and chop roughly. Thinly slice the sausages. Place the baked beans in a small saucepan with the tomato ketchup, sausage and eggs. Heat through gently. Toast the bread and pile the bean mixture on top.

Potato and Sausage Salad
Serves 4: 300 calories per portion

575g (1¼ lb) new potatoes
30ml (2 tablespoons)
  oil-free French dressing
225g (8 oz) chipolata
  sausages
8 radishes
4 spring onions

60ml (4 tablespoons)
  low-calorie salad cream
60ml (4 tablespoons)
  natural yogurt
5ml (1 level teaspoon)
  French mustard
salt and pepper

Scrub the potatoes, then boil in their skins until tender. Drain and when they are just cool enough to handle remove skins and cut the potatoes into cubes. Toss in the oil-free French dressing. Grill the sausages. Cool and cut into slices. Top and tail the radishes. Discard tough green leaves and roots of spring onions. Thinly slice radishes and spring onions and add to the potatoes with the sausages. Mix together the low-calorie salad cream, yogurt and mustard and season with salt and pepper. Stir very gently into the salad, taking care not to break the potato.

Sausage Baked Potato
Serves 4: 310 calories per portion

4 potatoes, 200g (7 oz) each
225g (8 oz) pork sausages
60ml (4 level tablespoons) piccalilli

60ml (4 tablespoons) skimmed milk
salt and pepper

Scrub the potatoes, then bake in their jackets at 200°C (400°F), gas mark 6, for about 45 minutes or until soft when pinched. Cut in half lengthways and carefully scoop out the flesh leaving the shells intact. While the potatoes are cooking, grill the sausages thoroughly, then chop them. Mash the potato flesh with the piccalilli and skimmed milk. Season with salt and pepper, then stir in the chopped sausages. Pile back into the potato cases and reheat in the oven for about 10 minutes.

Sausage and Bean Hotpot
Serves 4: 355 calories per portion

340g (¾ lb) beef chipolata sausages
450g (1 lb) potatoes
1 medium onion
salt and pepper

450-g (15.9-oz) can baked beans with tomato sauce
284-g (10-oz) can low-calorie oxtail soup

Grill beef chipolata sausages. Slice the potatoes and onions and cook in boiling salted water until just tender. Drain and place half in a casserole dish. Cover with the sausages and top with remaining potatoes and onions. Season with salt and pepper. Mix together the baked beans and soup and pour over the top. Cover the dish and cook at 190°C (375°F), gas mark 5, for 20–25 minutes.

Sausage and Onion Bake
Serves 4: 370 calories per portion

450g (1 lb) pork sausages
1 packet Knorr Onion
  Sauce Mix
275ml (½ pint) skimmed
  milk

304-g (10.7-oz) can
  processed peas
2 tomatoes
25g (1 oz) fresh
  breadcrumbs

Grill the sausages well, then arrange in an ovenproof dish. Keep warm. Make up onion sauce mix using skimmed milk. Drain the peas and stir into sauce. Heat through and pour over the sausages. Slice the tomatoes and arrange on top. Sprinkle on the breadcrumbs and place under a low grill until the crumbs start to brown. Serve immediately.

HAM AND BACON MEALS

Spicy Bacon and Bean Toast
Serves 4: 225 calories per portion

2 bacon *or* ham picnic
　steaks, 100g (3½ oz)
　each
450-g (15.9-oz) can baked
　beans with tomato sauce
15ml (1 tablespoon)
　tomato ketchup

15ml (1 tablespoon)
　bottled brown sauce
4 slices bread from a large,
　medium-sliced loaf

Grill the bacon or ham picnic steaks. Discard any visible fat and cut the lean into cubes. Place in a saucepan with the baked beans, tomato ketchup and brown sauce. Heat through gently. Toast the bread and pile the bean mixture on top.

Cheese and Ham Toast
Serves 4: 300 calories per portion

175g (6 oz) Lancashire
　cheese
75g (3 oz) lean cooked
　ham
60ml (4 tablespoons)
　tomato ketchup

salt and pepper
4 slices bread from a large,
　medium-sliced loaf

Grate the Lancashire cheese or crumble it finely. Discard all visible fat from the ham and chop the lean. Mix together the cheese, ham and ketchup. Season with salt and pepper. Toast the bread on one side only. Spread the untoasted sides with the cheese mixture. Grill until melted and starting to change colour.

Eggs Maryland
Serves 4: 300 calories per portion

4 eggs, size 3
125g (4 oz) lean cooked
  ham
198-g (7-oz) can sweetcorn
  kernels
30ml (2 level tablespoons)
  cornflour
275ml (½ pint) skimmed
  milk

75g (3 oz) mature Cheddar
  cheese
salt, pepper and a little
  mustard
30ml (2 level tablespoons)
  fresh breadcrumbs

Hardboil the eggs for 10 minutes and then cool in cold water. Shell, halve and place in an ovenproof dish. Discard all visible fat from the ham and chop the lean. Drain the sweetcorn. Blend the cornflour with a little of the skimmed milk until smooth and then add the remaining milk. Pour into a saucepan and bring to the boil, stirring all the time and simmer for 2 minutes. Grate the cheese and add two thirds to the sauce with the ham and corn. Season to taste with salt, pepper and a little mustard and pour over the eggs. Sprinkle the remaining cheese and the breadcrumbs on top and reheat in the oven at 190°C (375°F), gas mark 5, for about 15 minutes.

Ham and Fruit Slaw with bread
Serves 4: 325 calories per portion

225g (8 oz) cooked ham,
  preferably thickly sliced
227-g (8-oz) can pineapple
  in natural juice
225g (8 oz) white cabbage
125g (4 oz) carrot
3 sticks celery
25g (1 oz) raisins

120ml (8 tablespoons)
  low-calorie salad cream
salt and pepper
4 slices bread from a
  large, medium-sliced
  loaf
25g (1 oz) low-fat spread

Discard all visible fat from the ham and cut the lean into
small pieces. Drain the pineapple (give the juice to
someone in the family to drink) and cut into chunks.
Shred the cabbage, grate the carrot and roughly chop the
celery. Mix together the ham, pineapple, cabbage, carrot,
celery and low-calorie salad cream. Season with salt and
pepper. Spread the bread with the low-fat spread and
serve with the salad.

Ham and Vegetable Pie
Serves 4: 330 calories per portion

350g (12 oz) carrots
225g (8 oz) mushrooms
450g (1 lb) frozen broad
  beans
225g (8 oz) lean cooked
  ham, thickly sliced
2 packets Colman's
  Parsley Sauce Mix

568ml (1 pint) skimmed
  milk
salt and pepper
25g (1 oz) Edam cheese
50g (2 oz) fresh
  breadcrumbs

Slice the carrots and cook in boiling salted water for 15 minutes. Slice the mushrooms and add to the pan with the broad beans. Cook for 5 minutes longer. Discard all visible fat from the ham and cube the lean. Make up the parsley sauce mix using the skimmed milk, then stir in the ham and vegetables. Heat through over a low heat, stirring all the time. Season with salt and pepper and turn into a warm ovenproof dish. Grate the Edam cheese and sprinkle on top with the breadcrumbs. Grill until the cheese melts and the breadcrumbs start to brown.

Yorkshire Rarebit
Serves 4: 350 calories per portion

150g (5 oz) Lancashire cheese

4 eggs, size 3
4 slices bread from a large, medium-sliced loaf

125g (4 oz) lean cooked ham

Grate or crumble the cheese. Poach the eggs in water or in a non-stick pan. While they are poaching toast the bread on one side only. Cover the untoasted sides with cheese and grill until melted. Discard all visible fat from the ham and place the lean on the cheese. Heat under the grill and place eggs on top. Serve straight away.

Bean, Egg and Potato Grill
Serves 4: 440 calories per portion

4 rashers streaky bacon
1 large packet Cadbury's Smash
4 eggs, size 3

2 425-g (15-oz) cans baked beans with tomato sauce
50g (2 oz) Edam cheese

Grill the bacon until crisp, then break into small pieces. Make up the Smash as instructed and stir in the bacon. Spread the mixture over the base and sides of a fireproof dish and keep warm. Poach the eggs and heat the baked beans. Spread the beans over the potato and arrange the eggs on top. Grate the cheese and sprinkle over the eggs. Grill until the cheese melts.

FISH MEALS

Crispy Topped Cod
Serves 4: 180 calories per portion

4 Birds Eye Cod, Coley, Haddock Steaks
2.5ml (½ teaspoon) oil
45ml (3 level tablespoons) dried breadcrumbs
45ml (3 tablespoons) tomato ketchup
1.25ml (¼ teaspoon) Worcestershire sauce
salt and pepper
50g (2 oz) Cheddar cheese

Brush the fish steaks with oil and grill until just cooked, turning once. Mix together the breadcrumbs, tomato ketchup and Worcestershire sauce. Season with salt and pepper and spread over the fish. Grate the cheese and sprinkle on top. Grill under a low heat for 4–5 minutes.

Baked Potato with Herring Roes
Serves 4: 210 calories per portion

4 potatoes, 175g (6 oz)   squeeze lemon juice
  each   salt and pepper
225g (8 oz) soft herring   watercress
  roes
90ml (6 tablespoons)
  Silver Top milk

Scrub the potatoes, then bake in their jackets at 200°C
(400°F), gas mark 6, for about 45 minutes or until soft
when pinched. Cut in half lengthways and carefully scoop
out the flesh, leaving the skins intact. Place the herring
roes in a small saucepan with the milk. Cover with a
close-fitting lid and simmer gently for 10 minutes. (If the
pan lid does not fit tightly place a piece of foil on top of
the pan.) Turn the roes into a basin with the milk. Add
a squeeze of lemon juice and mash well. Season with salt
and pepper and pile back into the potato cases. Reheat in
the oven for 10 minutes. Garnish with watercress.

Scrambled Egg with Kipper on Toast
Serves 4: 245 calories per portion

170-g (6-oz) packet Findus   salt and pepper
  Kipper Fillets   4 slices bread from a large,
4 eggs, size 3   medium-sliced loaf

Cook the kippers in the bag as instructed. Remove from
the bag and reserve the liquid. Skin and flake the kipper
fillets. Lightly beat the eggs with the kipper liquid and
season with salt and pepper. Stir in the flaked kipper.

Cook in a non-stick pan over a low heat, stirring all the time, until creamy. While the eggs are cooking toast the bread. Serve scrambled eggs on the toast.

Smoked Haddock and Butter Bean Salad
Serves 4: 255 calories per portion

450g (1 lb) smoked
  haddock or cod fillet

2 eggs, size 3

450-g (15.9-oz) can butter
  beans

90ml (6 tablespoons)
  natural yogurt

15ml (1 tablespoon) lemon
  juice

1.25–2.5ml (¼–½ level
  teaspoon) curry powder

15ml (1 level tablespoon)
  chopped parsley

salt and pepper

lettuce

Poach the smoked haddock or cod in water until it flakes easily – about 10–15 minutes. Drain; remove bones and skin and flake roughly. Hardboil the eggs and cool in cold water. Drain butter beans and mix with the fish. Blend together the yogurt, lemon juice, curry powder and parsley. The amount of curry powder can vary according to taste; the finished dressing should be fairly mild. Mix the fish and butter beans with the dressing and season to taste with salt and pepper. The fish may be salty enough without extra salt. Arrange some lettuce leaves on a serving dish and pile the fish and bean mixture on top. Slice the eggs and arrange on top.

Baked Potato with Sild
Serves 4: 270 calories per portion

4 potatoes, 175g (6 oz)   113g (4 oz) carton cottage
  each   cheese with chives
2 106-g (3¾ oz) cans sild   salt and pepper
  in tomato sauce

Scrub the potatoes, then bake in their jackets at 200°C
(400°F), gas mark 6, for about 45 minutes or until soft
when pinched. Cut in half lengthways and scoop out the
flesh leaving the shells intact. Mash the flesh with the sild
and their sauce and the cottage cheese. Season with salt
and pepper. Pile back into the cases. Reheat in the oven
for about 10 minutes.

Crunchy Fish Pie
Serves 4: 270 calories per portion

4 Birds Eye Cod, Coley,   15ml (1 tablespoon)
  Haddock *or* Hake   skimmed milk
  Steaks   75g (3 oz) Cheddar cheese
295-g (10.4-oz) Campbell's   50g (2 oz) fresh
  Condensed Cream of   breadcrumbs
  Mushroom Soup

Thaw the fish steaks and place in a shallow ovenproof
dish. Mix the soup and milk together and spread over the
fish. Grate the cheese, mix with the breadcrumbs and
sprinkle on top. Bake at 190°C (375°F), gas mark 5, for
20–25 minutes.

Seafood Pizza
Serves 4: 280 calories per portion

125g (4 oz) self-raising
  flour
2.5ml (1/2 level teaspoon)
  baking powder
2.5ml (1/2 level teaspoon)
  dry mustard powder
2.5ml (1/2 level teaspoon)
  salt
2.5ml (1/2 level teaspoon)
  mixed dried herbs

25g (1 oz) butter
75–90ml (5–6 tablespoons)
  skimmed milk
4 tomatoes
198-g (7-oz) can tuna in
  brine
50g (2 oz) peeled prawns
50g (2 oz) Edam cheese

Sieve together the flour, baking powder, dry mustard and
salt. Add herbs and rub in the butter. Mix in enough
skimmed milk to make a soft, scone-type dough. Place on
a lightly greased baking sheet and pat into an 8- to 9-inch
round. Slice the tomatoes and arrange on top. Drain and
flake the tuna and spread over the tomatoes. Sprinkle on
the prawns and grated cheese and bake for 20–25 minutes
at 200°C (400°F), gas mark 6. Serve hot or cold.

Fish Pie
Serves 4: 340 calories per portion

225g (8 oz) smoked cod *or*
  haddock fillet
225g (8 oz) cod *or* haddock
  fillet
275ml (1/2 pint) skimmed
  milk
2 eggs, size 3

125g (4 oz) frozen peas
1 packet Colman's Parsley
  Sauce Mix
salt and pepper
1 large packet Cadbury's
  Smash
25g (1 oz) Cheddar cheese

Place all the fish in a shallow saucepan with the milk. Cover the pan and simmer gently for 15 minutes. While the fish is cooking, hardboil the eggs for 8 minutes, then place in a bowl of cold water to cool. Cook the peas as instructed. Drain fish, reserving the milk. Skin and flake the fish. Shell and roughly chop the eggs. Measure the reserved milk and if necessary make up to 275ml (1/2 pint) with a little water. If there is more than 275ml (1/2 pint) discard the excess. Use the milk to make up the packet sauce mix as instructed, then mix in the flaked fish, chopped eggs and peas. Season with a little pepper and some salt if necessary. The smoked fish may have made it salty enough. Turn into an ovenproof dish. Make up the Smash as instructed and spread over the fish mixture. Grate the cheese and sprinkle on top. Bake at 200°C (400°F), gas mark 6, for 25–30 minutes.

Smoky Fish Pie
Serves 4: 415 calories per portion

575g (1¼ lb) smoked
  haddock *or* cod fillet
425ml (¾ pint) skimmed
  milk
1 bay leaf
pepper
450g (1 lb) frozen mixed
  vegetables

salt
40g (1½ oz) low-fat spread
40g (1½ oz) flour
75g (3 oz) fresh
  breadcrumbs
40g (1½ oz) Cheddar
  cheese

Place the smoked fish in a saucepan with the milk and bay leaf. Season with pepper. Cover the pan and poach gently until the fish flakes easily – about 10 minutes. Discard the bay leaf. Remove fish from the pan and discard the skin and bones. Flake the fish. Cook the vegetables as instructed; drain and set aside. Add low-fat spread and flour to the milk in the saucepan, then bring to the boil, whisking all the time. Simmer for 1 minute. Add fish and vegetables and season with salt and more pepper, if necessary. It may not need any salt if the fish is salty. Turn into an ovenproof dish and sprinkle the breadcrumbs and cheese on top. Bake at 190°C (375°F), gas mark 5, for 20 minutes.

VEGETARIAN MEALS

Spanish Omelette
Serves 4: 150 calories per portion

75g (3 oz) boiled *or* canned, drained potatoes
1 spring onion
50g (2 oz) canned pimento
1 tomato
4 eggs, size 3
salt and pepper
10ml (2 teaspoons) oil
25g (1 oz) boiled *or* canned, drained sweetcorn
25g (1 oz) boiled *or* canned, drained peas

Cut the potato into cubes. Discard tough green leaves and roots from spring onions, then slice bulb. Dice pimento. Skin and roughly chop tomato. Lightly beat eggs together and season with salt and pepper. Heat oil in a non-stick omelette pan and cook potato and spring onions over the heat until the potato starts to brown. Add the sweetcorn, peas, pimento and tomato. Pour in the egg and cook over a moderate heat until the base is set. Tilt and gently shake the pan so that the runny mixture goes underneath. Grill until the top sets and then slide onto a plate. The omelette is served flat. It should not be folded. Cut into four and serve immediately.

Cauliflower Cheese
Serves 4: 175 calories per portion

900g (2 lb) cauliflower	2.5ml (½ level teaspoon)
25g (1 oz) powdered	made mustard
skimmed milk	salt and pepper
25g (1 oz) cornflour	15ml (1 level tablespoon)
75g (3 oz) Cheddar cheese	fresh breadcrumbs

Discard tough leaves and stem from cauliflower, then cook in boiling salted water until just tender. Drain and reserve 275ml (½ pint) liquid. Place cauliflower in an ovenproof dish and keep warm. Let reserved liquid cool very slightly, then whisk in powdered skimmed milk. Blend a little of this liquid with the cornflour until smooth. Add the remaining liquid and pour into a saucepan. Bring to the boil, stirring continuously and cook for 2 minutes. Grate cheese and add two thirds to the sauce with the mustard. Season and pour over the cauliflower. Sprinkle the remaining cheese and breadcrumbs on top, then heat under the grill until the cheese melts and starts to brown.

Cauliflower and Potato Soufflé
Serves 4: 225 calories per portion

5ml (1 level teaspoon)
  butter
225g (8 oz) cauliflower
  florets
225g (8 oz) potato,
  weighed peeled

60ml (4 tablespoons) milk
3 eggs, size 3
75g (3 oz) strong Cheddar
  cheese
salt and pepper

Preheat oven to 200°C (400°F), gas mark 6. Grease a 7- or 8-inch soufflé dish with the butter. Discard any tough stem and leaves from the cauliflower, and then boil the florets until tender. Drain and mash. Boil the potato until tender. Drain and mash with the milk. Add the cauliflower. Separate the eggs and grate the cheese. Beat the yolks and cheese into the vegetables and season well with salt and pepper. Whisk the egg whites until stiff but not dry and then fold a quarter into the vegetables. Gently fold in the remaining egg whites and turn into the prepared dish. Bake for 35 minutes until risen and lightly coloured on top. Serve immediately.

Note Do not open the oven door while the soufflé is cooking or it may collapse.

Curried Scrambled Eggs on Toast
Serves 4: 245 calories per portion

6 eggs, size 3
60ml (4 tablespoons)
  skimmed milk
1 medium onion
15g (½ oz) butter

5ml (1 level teaspoon)
  curry powder
salt and pepper
4 slices bread from a large,
  medium-sliced loaf

Lightly beat the eggs and skimmed milk together. Finely chop the onion. Melt the butter in a saucepan, preferably a non-stick pan, add the onion and cook gently until soft. Stir in the curry powder and cook for a further 2 minutes. Add the eggs and cook over a low heat, stirring all the time, until creamy. Toast the bread and pile the eggs on top.

Tomato and Onion Scramble on Toast
Serves 4: 245 calories per portion

1 small onion	1.25ml (¼ level teaspoon)
2 tomatoes	mixed dried herbs
6 eggs, size 3	15g (½ oz) butter
60ml (4 tablespoons)	4 slices bread from a large,
skimmed milk	medium-sliced loaf
salt and pepper	

Finely chop the onion. Roughly chop the tomatoes. Lightly beat the eggs and skimmed milk together and season with salt and pepper and herbs. Melt the butter in a non-stick saucepan; add the onion and cook until soft. Add the eggs and tomato and cook over a low heat, stirring continuously, until creamy. Toast the bread and serve the egg mixture on top.

Cheese and Tomato Pizza
Serves 4: 265 calories per portion

125g (4 oz) self-raising
  flour
2.5ml (½ level teaspoon)
  baking powder
2.5ml (½ level teaspoon)
  dry mustard
2.5ml (½ level teaspoon)
  salt
2.5ml (½ level teaspoon)
  mixed dried herbs
1 small onion

25g (1 oz) butter *or*
  margarine
60ml (4 tablespoons)
  skimmed milk
30ml (2 level tablespoons)
  tomato ketchup
4 tomatoes
1.25ml (¼ level teaspoon)
  dried basil *or* mixed
  dried herbs
75g (3 oz) Cheddar cheese

Sieve together the flour, baking powder, dry mustard and salt. Add the mixed dried herbs and rub in the butter or margarine. Grate the onion and add to dry mixture with the milk to make a soft, scone-type dough. Place on a lightly greased baking sheet and pat out into an 8- to 9-inch round. Spread with the tomato ketchup. Slice the tomatoes and arrange on top and sprinkle with basil or mixed herbs. Grate the cheese and sprinkle on top. Bake at 200°C (400°F), gas mark 6, for 20–25 minutes. Serve hot or cold.

Egg Mornay
Serves 4: 280 calories per portion

4 eggs, size 3	salt, pepper and a pinch
50g (2 oz) mature Cheddar	dry mustard
cheese	little paprika, optional
20g (3/4 oz) low-fat spread	4 slices bread from a large,
20g (3/4 oz) plain flour	medium-sliced loaf
215ml (7½ fl. oz)	
skimmed milk	

Hardboil the eggs. While they are cooking, make the sauce. Grate the cheese. Place low-fat spread, flour and skimmed milk in a saucepan and bring to the boil, whisking continuously. Simmer for 1 minute. Add the cheese and season with salt, pepper and a pinch of dry mustard. Shell the eggs and cut in half. Arrange on a serving dish and pour the sauce over. Sprinkle with a little paprika, if liked. Toast the bread, cut into triangles and arrange around the eggs.

Cheese and Pickle Toast
Serves 4: 285 calories per portion

175g (6 oz) Cheddar	45ml (3 level tablespoons)
cheese	Branston pickle
4 slices bread from a large,	2 tomatoes
medium-sliced loaf	3 spring onions

Grate the Cheddar cheese. Toast the bread and spread with pickle. Slice the tomatoes. Discard the tough green stems from spring onions and chop the white part. Arrange tomatoes and spring onions on top of the pickle.

Sprinkle cheese on top. Grill gently until cheese melts and the topping is heated through.

Egg Curry with Rice
Serves 4: 325 calories per portion

1 medium onion
1 clove garlic, optional
10ml (1 teaspoon) oil
7g (¼ oz) butter
10ml (2 level teaspoons)
　curry powder
575ml (1 pint) water
1 chicken stock cube
60ml (4 level tablespoons)
　tomato chutney
salt and pepper
30ml (2 level tablespoons)
　cornflour
4 eggs, size 3
175g (6 oz) long-grain rice

Finely chop the onion and crush the garlic if used. Heat the oil in a saucepan, add the butter to melt and then add the onion and garlic. Cook over a low heat until the onion is soft. Add the curry powder and cook over a low heat for 2 minutes, stirring all the time. Add the water, crumbled stock cube and tomato chutney. Season with salt and pepper and bring to the boil, stirring. Cover the pan and simmer for 15 minutes. While the sauce is cooking, hardboil the eggs for 8 minutes and boil the rice as instructed on the packet. Drain the rice and keep warm. Blend the cornflour with a little cold water and add to the sauce. Bring to the boil, stirring continuously and simmer for 1–2 minutes. Shell the eggs, add to the sauce and heat through. Serve on the rice.

Puddings to Share

If you are lunching on your own the best pudding to choose is a piece of fresh fruit or a small flavoured or low-fat natural yogurt. We have included a list of the calorie values of these in the chart on page 145. But if your family usually demand that the evening meal or Sunday lunch is followed by something sweet, why not try some of the following desserts on them? You can then have a quarter portion without damaging your dieting campaign or feeling deprived.

If you usually dish up jam roly poly or chocolate sponge pudding with chocolate sauce, a portion could be costing you around 500 calories. None of the puddings here costs more than 195 calories a portion.

We have used ice cream in some of the recipes and this makes an excellent low-calorie dessert on its own. Despite its name, even dairy ice cream is much lower in fat than many people imagine. And the ingredients are whisked up and frozen to trap in lots of no-calorie air. Most of the popular brands of ice cream work out at around 50 calories an ounce (a small ice cream scoop holds about 1½ oz when rounded). Try experimenting with some fresh fruit and ice cream mixtures yourself. Not only will you save calories, you'll also spend less time slaving over a hot stove.

Raspberry Sundae
Serves 4: 125 calories per portion

225g (8 oz) raspberries, fresh *or* frozen and thawed

20ml (4 level teaspoons) caster sugar

30ml (2 level tablespoons) chopped nuts

1 Lyons Maid Handy Pack *or* 1 Walls Popular Pack Raspberry Ripple Ice Cream

Place half the raspberries in the base of four sundae glasses. Purée the remaining raspberries in a blender with the sugar or rub through a sieve and stir in the sugar. Divide the ice cream into four and place on the raspberries. Top with the raspberry sauce and sprinkle with the nuts.

Raspberry Yogurt Brûlée
Serves 4: 125 calories per portion

450g (1 lb) raspberries, fresh *or* frozen, thawed
2 individual cartons raspberry yogurt
30ml (2 level tablespoons) soft brown sugar

Divide the raspberries between four ramekins or individual ovenproof dishes and cover with the yogurt. Sprinkle on the sugar and grill until it melts. Serve immediately.

Fresh Fruit Salad with Cream
Serves 4: 130 calories per portion

1 medium orange
125g (4 oz) black grapes
125g (4 oz) strawberries (if fresh are not available, use frozen)
1 medium apple

1 medium peach *or* 1 small pear
1 small banana
225ml (8 fl. oz) apple juice
125ml (4 fl. oz) half cream

Peel and segment the orange. Cut each segment in half. Halve and pip the grapes. If the strawberries are large, cut in halves or quarters. If they are small, leave whole. Quarter and core the apple and then cut into slices. Halve the peach or pear and remove the stone or core. Cut into cubes. Peel and slice the banana. Mix all the fruits with the apple juice and serve with the cream.

Baked Bananas
Serves 4: 135 calories per portion

4 medium bananas
60ml (4 tablespoons) pineapple juice

50g (2 oz) sultanas
15g (1/2 oz) hazelnuts

Peel the bananas and cut into slices. Place in an ovenproof dish with the pineapple juice and mix well so that all the pieces of banana are coated. Sprinkle on the sultanas. Cover the dish with a lid or foil and bake at 180°C (350°F), gas mark 4, for 20 minutes. Place the hazelnuts on a baking sheet and cook in the oven at the same time until golden. Rub the skins off the hazelnuts with a piece of kitchen paper. Chop roughly and sprinkle over the bananas. Serve immediately.

Baked Apples with Raisins
Serves 4: 135 calories per portion

4 cooking apples, 175g (6 oz) each

60ml (4 tablespoons) apple juice

20ml (4 level teaspoons) brown sugar

75g (3 oz) raisins

Core the cooking apples and make a cut through the skin around the middle. Place them in an ovenproof dish and fill the cavities with the raisins and brown sugar. Spoon over the apple juice and bake at 190°C (375°F), gas mark 5 for 35–45 minutes.

Ice Cream with Hot Cherry Sauce
Serves 4: 140 calories per portion

405-g (14.29-oz) jar Batchelors Cherry Pack-A-Pie
1 Handy Pack Lyons Maid Vanilla Ice Cream *or* 1
  Popular Brick Walls Golden Vanilla Ice Cream

Gently heat the pie filling in a saucepan. Cut the ice cream into four and place in individual dishes. Pour over the hot cherry pie filling and serve immediately.

Rhubarb and Orange Fluff
Serves 4: 150 calories per portion

450g (1 lb) rhubarb   25g (1 oz) powdered
150ml (¼ pint) water   skimmed milk
1 packet orange jelly cubes
individual carton orange
  yogurt

Cut the rhubarb into slices and place in a saucepan with
the water. Cook over a low heat until tender. Remove from
the heat. Cut the jelly into cubes and add to the hot
rhubarb. Stir until dissolved. Place in an electric blender
with the yogurt and powdered skimmed milk and blend
until smooth. If no blender is available rub the rhubarb
and juices through a sieve and then add the yogurt and
powdered skimmed milk which has been mixed with a
very small amount of water. Chill until on the point of
setting. Whisk until light and fluffy. Turn into a serving
dish and chill until set.

Hazelnut and Banana Brûlée
Serves 4: 160 calories per portion

4 small bananas
2 individual cartons hazelnut yogurt
30ml (2 level tablespoons) soft brown sugar

Peel and slice the bananas and mix with the yogurt. Divide
between four ramekins or individual ovenproof dishes and
sprinkle the sugar on top. Cook under a hot grill until the
sugar melts. Serve immediately.

Raspberry Mousse
Serves 4: 165 calories per portion

1 packet raspberry jelly
boiling water
225g (8 oz) raspberries,
   fresh *or* frozen, thawed

1 small can evaporated
   milk, chilled

Make the jelly up to 275ml (½ pint) with boiling water.
Stir until the jelly is all dissolved. Leave until cold and
beginning to set. Purée the raspberries in a blender or rub
through a sieve. Whisk into the setting jelly and continue
whisking until frothy. Whisk the evaporated milk until
thick and creamy and then fold into the jelly. Pour into
four serving dishes and leave until set.

Peach Melba
Serves 4: 165 calories per portion

225g (8 oz) fresh *or* frozen,
   thawed raspberries
25g (1 oz) caster sugar
8 drained, canned peach
   halves

1 Handy Pack Lyons
Maid Vanilla Ice Cream
or 1 Popular Brick Walls
Golden Vanilla Ice
Cream

Purée the raspberries in a blender with the sugar or rub
through a sieve and then stir in the sugar. Cut the ice
cream into four pieces and place each in a serving dish.
Top each piece of ice cream with two peach halves and
spoon over the sauce. Serve immediately.

Apple and Apricot Meringue
Serves 4: 170 calories per portion

125g (4 oz) dried apricots	2 egg whites
450g (1 lb) cooking apples	50g (2 oz) caster sugar
15ml (1 level tablespoon) honey	

Soak the dried apricots in water for several hours or overnight. Drain and place in a saucepan with 60ml (4 tablespoons) of the soaking liquid. Discard the remaining liquid. Peel, core and slice the apples and add to the saucepan. Cover and cook over a low heat until the fruits are soft. Stir in the honey and turn into an ovenproof dish. Whisk the egg whites until stiff. Add the caster sugar and whisk until stiff again. Pile on top of the apple mixture and bake at 190°C (375°F), gas mark 5, for 10–15 minutes or until the meringue starts to brown. Serve hot.

Trifle
Serves 4: 180 calories per portion

2 trifle sponges	20ml (4 level teaspoons) sugar
10ml (2 level teaspoons) jam	425ml (¾ pint) skimmed milk
411-g (14½-oz) can fruit salad *or* fruit cocktail in natural juice *or* low-calorie syrup	30ml (2 level tablespoons) flaked almonds
30ml (2 level tablespoons) custard powder	

Cut the trifle sponges in half, then sandwich together again with the jam. Cut each sponge into four and place in the base of a serving bowl. Drain the fruit salad or fruit cocktail and reserve 30ml (2 tablespoons) juice. Sprinkle this over the sponges and arrange the fruit around the edge. Blend the custard powder and sugar with a little skimmed milk until smooth. Heat the remaining milk to boiling point and pour onto the custard mixture, stirring all the time. Return to the pan and bring to the boil, stirring continuously until thickened. Pour over the fruit and sponge and leave to cool. Grill the flaked almonds until golden, watching them all the time to make sure they do not burn. Sprinkle over the trifle just before serving.

Apple Crisp
Serves 4: 190 calories per portion

675g (1½ lb) cooking apples	50g (2 oz) cornflakes
30ml (2 tablespoons) water	50g (2 oz) muesli
25g (1 oz) fruit sugar (e.g., Dietade)	

Peel, core and slice the cooking apples and place in a saucepan with the water. Cover and cook gently until soft. Stir in two-thirds of the fruit sugar and place in an ovenproof dish. Crush the cornflakes and mix with the muesli and remaining fruit sugar. Sprinkle over the apples and bake at 190°C (375°F), gas mark 5, for 15 minutes. Serve hot.

Banana Split
Serves 4: 195 calories per portion

4 small bananas	60ml (4 level tablespoons)
1 Lyons Maid Handy	Colmans *or* HP *or* Jiff *or*
Pack Vanilla Ice Cream	Lyons Maid Chocolate
or 1 Popular Brick Walls	Dessert Sauce
Golden Vanilla Ice	30ml (2 level tablespoons)
Cream	chopped mixed nuts

Peel the bananas and cut in half lengthwise. Cut the ice cream into four. Place a piece of ice cream and a split banana on four individual serving dishes. Spoon over the sauce and sprinkle on the nuts. Serve immediately.

Nibbles and Snacks

Stop thinking that you are 'bad' or have no willpower if you have a tendency to nibble during the day. It is a very natural urge. You only have to look at the growth of snack foods over the last few years to realize that food manufacturers have recognized that snacking is very common and have produced goods to fill the gaps between main meals.

If you are a nibbler, then your best plan when dieting is to allow for some little extras in your calorie allowance. In this section we have devised a number of very low-calorie nibbles which can be made in minutes. When the children arrive home from school demanding something to eat, it can be very difficult to resist joining them. If this is a time when you usually succumb to temptation, plan to eat a crispbread snack.

One of the great disadvantages of being at home all day with the kitchen so handy is that there is nothing to prevent you raiding the larder whenever you like. So in this chapter we have also included some munch-box nibbles and vegetables with spicy dips which you can make up in the morning and 'raid' whenever you like during the day. Just count the total into your daily allowance and you can nibble away without those horrid feelings of guilt and failure that come from bingeing on forbidden fancies.

Salmon and Cheese Tomatoes
Serves 1: 25 calories

1 medium tomato
15ml (1 level tablespoon) Eden Vale Cottage Cheese
    with Salmon and Cucumber

Cut the tomato in half and scoop out the pips and flesh.
Discard the pips. Chop the flesh and mix with the cottage
cheese. Pile back into the tomato case and serve.

Cheese and Celery Sticks
Serves 1: 30 calories

1 large stick celery
Marmite *or* yeast extract
15ml (1 level tablespoon) curd cheese

Spread the hollow of the celery stick with a little Marmite
or yeast extract. Fill with the curd cheese and cut into four
pieces.

Cheese and Pickled Onion Crispbread
Serves 1: 40 calories

1 Energen *or* Krispen crispbread
5ml (1 level teaspoon) Cheddar cheese spread
1 pickled onion

Spread the crispbread with Cheddar cheese spread. Slice
the pickled onion and arrange on top.

Curd Cheese and Gherkin Crispbread
Serves 1: 40 calories

1 Energen *or* Krispen crispbread
1 gherkin
15ml (1 level tablespoon) curd cheese

Chop the gherkin and mix with the curd cheese. Spread on the crispbread.

Beef and Mango Chutney Crispbread
Serves 1: 40 calories

1 Energen *or* Krispen crispbread
5ml (1 level teaspoon) beef spread
5ml (1 level teaspoon) mango chutney
little red *or* green pepper

Spread the crispbread with the beef spread and top with the chutney. Arrange a little pepper on top.

Chicken and Corn Relish Crispbread
Serves 1: 40 calories

1 Energen *or* Krispen crispbread
5ml (1 level teaspoon) chicken spread
10ml (2 level teaspoons) corn relish

Spread the crispbread with the chicken spread and top with the corn relish.

Cheese Salad Crispbread
Serves 1: 40 calories

1 Energen *or* Krispen
 crispbread
5ml (1 level teaspoon)
 cheese spread with
 chives *or* onion

2–3 slices tomato
2–3 slices cucumber

Spread the crispbread with the flavoured cheese spread and top with the tomato and cucumber.

Cheese and Gherkin Topped Cucumber Slices
Serves 1: 40 calories

2 small gherkins
30ml (2 level tablespoons) cottage cheese with prawns
6 slices cucumber

Chop the gherkins and mix with the cottage cheese and prawns. Divide this topping between the cucumber slices.

Pineapple and Cheese Snack
Serves 1: 40 calories

1 ring pineapple, canned
 in natural juice, drained
1 lettuce leaf

15ml (1 level tablespoon)
 curd cheese
1 toasted hazelnut

Place the pineapple ring on the lettuce leaf. Fill the hole with the curd cheese. Roughly chop the hazelnut and sprinkle on top.

Fish Paste, Tomato and Olive Crispbread
Serves 1: 45 calories

1 Energen *or* Krispen   1 small tomato
   crispbread   1 stuffed olive
5ml (1 level teaspoon) fish
   paste

Spread the crispbread with the fish paste. Slice the tomato
and olive and arrange on top.

Jam Crispbread
Serves 1: 45 calories

1 Energen *or* Krispen crispbread
2.5ml (½ level teaspoon) low-fat spread
5ml (1 level teaspoon) jam

Spread the crispbread with the low-fat spread and then
with the jam.

Fish and Cheese Crispbread
Serves 1: 45 calories

1 Energen *or* Krispen   15ml (1 level tablespoon)
   crispbread   cottage cheese
5ml (1 level teaspoon) crab   3 slices cucumber
   or salmon paste

Spread the crispbread firstly with the fish paste and then
with the cottage cheese. Top with the slices of cucumber.

Cheese and Pickle Crispbread
Serves 1: 45 calories

1 Energen *or* Krispen crispbread
1/2 triangle cheese spread, 7g (1/4 oz)
5ml (1 level teaspoon) Branston-type pickle

Spread the crispbread with the cheese spread and top with
the pickle.

Blue Cheese and Tomato Chutney Crispbread
Serves 1: 45 calories

1 Energen *or* Krispen crispbread
5ml (1 level teaspoon) blue cheese spread
5ml (1 level teaspoon) tomato chutney

Spread the crispbread with the blue cheese spread and top
with the tomato chutney.

Curd Cheese and Cucumber Relish Crispbread
Serves 1: 50 calories

1 Energen *or* Krispen crispbread
15ml (1 level tablespoon) curd cheese
10ml (2 level teaspoons) cucumber relish

Spread the crispbread with the curd cheese and top with
the cucumber relish.

Blue Cheese and Celery Sticks
Serves 1: 55 calories

1 large stick celery
15ml (1 level tablespoon) blue cheese spread

Fill the hollow of the celery stick with the blue cheese spread and cut into four pieces.

Strawberry Yogurt Treat
Serves 1: 55 calories

75g (3 oz) fresh strawberries
10ml (2 teaspoons) unsweetened orange juice
45g (3 level tablespoons) natural yogurt

Slice the strawberries and mix with the orange juice and yogurt.

Ham and Vegetable Crispbread
Serves 1: 60 calories

15g (½ oz) lean cooked ham
15ml (1 level tablespoon) Waistline Low-Calorie Country Vegetable Spread
1 Energen *or* Krispen crispbread
2 slices tomato

Chop the ham and mix with the vegetable spread. Spread on the crispbread and top with the tomato.

Mincemeat and Grapefruit Grill
Serves 1: 60 calories

½ medium grapefruit
15g (½ oz) mincemeat

Loosen the segments of the grapefruit using a grapefruit knife or a small sharp knife. Spread the mincemeat on top and grill.

Egg Stuffed Tomato
Serves 1: 65 calories

1 medium tomato
½ hardboiled egg, size 3
15ml (1 level tablespoon) Waistline Country Vegetable
   Spread

Halve the tomato and scoop out the seeds and flesh. Discard the seeds. Chop the flesh, and the hardboiled egg. Mix with the Country Vegetable Spread and pile back into the tomato cases.

Melon with Raspberry Sauce
Serves 1: 65 calories

225g (8 oz) melon
50g (2 oz) fresh *or* frozen, thawed raspberries
5ml (1 level teaspoon) caster *or* icing sugar

Discard the skin from the melon and cut the flesh into cubes. Crush the raspberries and sugar together with a fork and spoon over the melon.

Spicy Vegetable and Egg Crispbread
Serves 1: 75 calories

1 Energen *or* Krispen crispbread
15ml (1 level tablespoon) Waistline Low-Calorie Spicy
    Vegetable Spread
½ hardboiled egg, size 3

Spread the crispbread with the spicy vegetable spread.
Slice the hardboiled egg and arrange on top.

Pineapple Yogurt Treat
Serves 1: 80 calories

2 rings pineapple canned   10ml (2 level teaspoons)
    in natural juice, drained   sultanas
10ml (2 teaspoons)   45ml (3 level tablespoons)
    pineapple juice from can   natural yogurt

Cut the pineapple into small pieces and mix with the juice,
sultanas and yogurt.

Cauliflower and Carrot Munch
80 calories

150g (5 oz) raw   1 sachet Knorr Salad
    cauliflower   Days, any flavour
150g (5 oz) raw carrots
60ml (4 tablespoons)
    oil-free French dressing

Discard tough leaves and stems from cauliflower and divide into sprigs. Cut carrot into small sticks. Whisk together oil-free French dressing and Salad Days, add the vegetables and mix well. Keep in a covered container in the refrigerator.

Instant Mini Cheesecake
Serves 1: 85 calories

1 medium digestive biscuit
10ml (2 level teaspoons) curd cheese
5ml (1 level teaspoon) jam

Spread biscuit with cheese and top with jam.

Red Cabbage and Leek Munch
140 calories

175g (6 oz) raw red cabbage
50g (2 oz) raw carrot
125g (4 oz) raw leek
30ml (2 tablespoons) oil-free French dressing
30ml (2 tablespoons) low-calorie salad cream
salt and pepper

Shred the red cabbage. Grate the carrot. Discard tough green leaves from leek and thinly slice white part. Divide into rings. Mix vegetables with dressings and season with salt and pepper. Keep in a covered container in the refrigerator.

Fruity Coleslaw Munch
200 calories

3 rings pineapple, canned
   in natural juice, drained
75g (3 oz) white cabbage
50g (2 oz) carrots
1 stick celery
30ml (2 level tablespoons)
   raisins or sultanas

30ml (2 tablespoons)
   natural yogurt
30ml (2 tablespoons)
   low-calorie salad cream
salt and pepper

Roughly chop the pineapple. Shred the cabbage, grate the carrot and thinly slice the celery. Mix all the ingredients together and season with salt and pepper. Keep in a covered container in the refrigerator.

Cooked Vegetable Munch
215 calories

75g (3 oz) cooked French
   beans *or* haricots verts
125g (4 oz) cooked frozen
   or canned sweetcorn
125g (4 oz) cooked peas

1/2 red pepper
30ml (2 tablespoons)
   Waistline Seafood Sauce
salt and pepper

Mix together the cold cooked vegetables. Discard pith and seeds from pepper and dice flesh. Mix all ingredients together and season with salt and pepper. Keep in a covered container in the refrigerator.

Grapefruit and Celery Munch
230 calories

2 fresh grapefruit   25g (1 oz) seedless raisins
2 sticks celery   15g (½ oz) flaked almonds

Peel and segment grapefruit, taking care to remove all white pith. Save juice to drink separately. Slice celery and mix with grapefruit segments, raisins and flaked almonds. Keep in a covered container.

Apricot and Cornflake Munch
250 calories

40g (1½ oz) cornflakes
25g (1 oz) dried apricots
30ml (2 level tablespoons) seedless raisins

Chop the dried apricots and mix with the cornflakes and raisins. Keep in a covered container in the refrigerator.

Fruit and Yogurt Munch
275 calories

125g (4 oz) fresh   individual carton natural
  strawberries   yogurt
125g (4 oz) black grapes   5ml (1 level teaspoon)
1 small banana   honey

Hull the strawberries and halve or quarter depending on size. Halve and pip grapes. Peel and thickly slice banana. Mix together yogurt and honey and then stir in fruit. Keep in a covered container in the refrigerator.

Rice Salad Munch
280 calories

50g (2 oz) long grain
 brown rice
45ml (3 tablespoons)
 oil-free French dressing
125g (4 oz) frozen peas

75g (3 oz) cucumber
1 stick celery
1/4 red *or* green pepper
salt and pepper

Boil the rice as instructed. Drain and while still hot stir in the oil-free French dressing. Boil the peas. Drain and rinse under cold water. Drain again and add to the rice. Dice the cucumber and celery. Discard white pith and seeds from pepper and dice flesh. Add cucumber, celery and pepper to rice and peas and season. Keep in a covered container in the refrigerator.

Bean Munch
300 calories

50g (2 oz) French beans *or*
 haricots verts
2 sticks celery
2 spring onions
223-g (7.9-oz) can red
 kidney beans

150-g (5.3-oz) can baked
 beans with tomato sauce
15ml (1 tablespoon)
 oil-free French dressing
salt and pepper

Boil the beans. Drain, refresh with cold running water and drain again. Chop celery. Discard roots and tough green leaves of spring onions and then chop bulbs. Drain red kidney beans. Mix all ingredients together and season with salt and pepper. Keep in a covered container in the refrigerator.

Crunchy Fruit Munch
315 calories

1 medium banana
1 medium apple
15ml (1 tablespoon) lemon
  juice

40g (1½ oz) Jordan's
  Original Crunchy

Peel and slice the banana. Core and dice the apple. Toss the fruits in the lemon juice and then drain well. Mix with the crunchy cereal and keep in a covered container.

Apple, Nut and Celery Munch
320 calories

25g (1 oz) hazelnuts
3 medium apples
lemon juice
4 sticks celery

60ml (4 tablespoons)
  natural yogurt
salt and pepper

Place the hazelnuts on the base of the grill pan and grill until they turn brown. Watch that they do not burn. Rub off the skins and roughly chop the nuts. Core and dice the apples and toss in a little lemon juice. Slice the celery. Mix all the ingredients together and season with salt and pepper.

Baking

If you can avoid baking while you are dieting, then your best plan is to do so. Home-baked pastries and cakes are usually high calorie and home baked bread is very much more tempting than the shop-bought varieties.

But if you really can't get out of doing some baking for the family (make sure it really is the family you are doing if for and not yourself) then the recipes in this chapter are the least fattening sort to bake. It is quite unrealistic to think you won't be tempted to sample some of your home-baked goodies, so allocate yourself a slice of cake or teabread and count the calories into your daily allowance.

All the sponges are made by the whisking method and do not contain fat, which is the highest calorie ingredient in a creamed-method sponge. And because you whisk in lots of air, you get a nice big slice for your calories. Whisk sponges have another advantage for a dieter. Although they can be frozen, they can't be kept sitting around in a cake tin for more than one day. So your best plan is to bake your cake just before it is due to be served. When you have eaten your allowance and the family have taken what they want, quickly put any leftovers into the freezer. The freezer, we find, stops that impulse binge because you have to wait for the goodie to defrost before you can proceed to eat it. And by then you may have overcome the urge.

The two teabread recipes also contain no fat and use dried fruit to add sweetness so that less sugar is needed. Don't worry that the artificial sweetener in one recipe will give your cake an artificial taste. In our tests we found it was quite undetectable. If other members of the family or tea-time guests would like to spread their teabread with butter or low-fat spread, they can do so but the teabread is very nice to eat without.

Sponge Sandwich
Makes 8 slices: 130 calories per slice

2.5ml (½ teaspoon) oil
3 eggs, size 3
75g (3 oz) caster sugar
75g (3 oz) plain flour

50g (2 oz) Robertson's
  Today's Recipe Jam
15ml (1 level tablespoon)
  icing sugar

Line the base of two 7-inch sandwich tins with greaseproof paper. Brush the sides and bases of the tins with the oil. Place the eggs and caster sugar in a large mixing bowl and stand it over a pan of water which is barely simmering. Whisk until thick and mousse-like. Remove bowl from pan and continue whisking for a few minutes longer. Sieve the flour over the surface of the egg mixture, then fold in very gently. Turn into the prepared tins and bake at 190°C (375°F), gas mark 5, for about 25 minutes or until well risen and golden brown. Turn out on to a wire rack to cool. Sandwich with the jam and dust the top with icing sugar.

Fairy Cakes
Makes 20: 70 calories each

3 eggs, size 3
75g (3 oz) caster sugar
75g (3 oz) plain flour
125g (4 oz) icing sugar
few drops colouring,
    optional

25ml (5 level teaspoons)
    hundreds and thousands
    or chocolate vermicelli
20 paper cake cases

Place the eggs and sugar in a large mixing bowl and stand
it over a pan of very gently simmering water. Whisk until
thick and mousse-like. Remove bowl from the pan and
whisk for a few minutes longer. Sieve the flour over the
surface of the egg mixture and fold in very gently. Stand
the paper cake cases on a baking sheet and divide the
sponge mixture between them. Bake at 190°C (375°F), gas
mark 5, for about 15 minutes or until risen and golden
brown. Cool on a wire rack. Sieve the icing sugar and mix
with enough warm water to make a coating consistency.
You will not need much water so add it very carefully, a
little at a time. Colour with a few drops of colouring if
liked and then spoon on to the cakes. Sprinkle on the
hundreds and thousands or vermicelli and leave until the
icing has set.

Swiss Roll
Makes 8 slices: 130 calories per slice

2.5ml (½ teaspoon) oil
3 eggs, size 3
75g (3 oz) caster sugar
plus 15ml (1 level
tablespoon)
75g (3 oz) plain flour

15ml (1 tablespoon) hot
water
50g (2 oz) Robertson's
Today's Recipe Jam,
any flavour

Line a swiss roll tin with greaseproof paper and brush with oil. Place the eggs and 75g (3 oz) caster sugar in a mixing bowl and stand it over a pan of very gently simmering water, whisking until thick and mousse-like. Remove the bowl from the pan and whisk for a few minutes longer. Sieve the flour over the surface of the egg mixture and fold in gently with the hot water. Turn into the prepared tin and bake at 220°C (425°F), gas mark 7 for 7–9 minutes or until well risen and golden brown. While sponge is baking, sprinkle a clean sheet of greaseproof paper with the 15ml (1 level tablespoon) caster sugar and gently warm the jam in a small saucepan (it should be warm not boiling). As soon as the cake is cooked, turn it out on to the paper and trim the edges. Spread with the jam. Make a cut halfway through the sponge one inch from the edge. Roll up using the paper to help get a firm roll. Cool on a wire rack still wrapped in the paper.

Fruit Tea Loaf
Makes 12 slices: 130 calories per slice

125g (4 oz) sultanas
125g (4 oz) currants
150ml (1/4 pint) hot tea
1 egg, size 3
grated rind 1/2 orange
90ml (6 tablespoons)
  orange juice
10ml (2 level teaspoons)
  baking powder

120ml (8 level
  tablespoons)
  Hermesetas Sprinkle
  Sweet
225g (8 oz) plain flour
1.25ml (1/4 level teaspoon)
  mixed spice
1.25ml (1/4 teaspoon) oil

Place the sultanas and currants in a basin and pour in the hot tea. Leave to soak for 4 hours or overnight. Lightly beat the egg and add to the fruit with the rind and juice of the orange and Hermesetas Sprinkle Sweet. Sieve together the flour, baking powder and mixed spice and then stir into the fruit mixture. Line a loaf tin with greaseproof paper and brush with the oil. Turn the mixture into the tin and bake at 180°C (350°F), gas mark 4, for 1 hour. Cool on a wire rack.

Note Guests and family can eat the loaf spread with butter if liked but this is not allowed for in the calories.

Chocolate and Orange Sponge Cake
Makes 8 slices: 140 calories per slice

2.5ml (1/2 teaspoon) oil
3 eggs, size 3
75g (3 oz) caster sugar
70g (2 1/2 oz) plain flour

15g (1/2 oz) cocoa
50g (2 oz) orange curd
15ml (1 level tablespoon)
  icing sugar

Line the base of two 7-inch sandwich tins with greaseproof paper and brush the paper and sides of the tins with oil. Place the eggs and caster sugar in a mixing bowl over a pan of very gently simmering water. Whisk until thick and mousse-like. Remove bowl from the pan and continue whisking for a few minutes. Sieve the flour and cocoa together over the surface of the egg mixture, then fold in gently. Turn into the prepared tins and bake at 190°C (375°F), gas mark 5, for about 25 minutes or until well risen. Turn out on to a wire rack and leave to cool. Sandwich the cakes together with the orange curd and dust the top with the icing sugar.

Bran Tea Loaf
Makes 12 slices: 160 calories per slice

75g (3 oz) All-Bran	175g (6 oz) self-raising
225g (8 oz) sultanas	flour
125g (4 oz) caster sugar	5ml (1 level teaspoon)
275ml (½ pint) skimmed	baking powder
milk	1.25ml (¼ teaspoon) oil

Place the All-Bran, sultanas, caster sugar and skimmed milk in a basin and stir well. Cover the basin and leave to soak in the refrigerator for several hours or overnight. Sieve the flour and baking powder together, then stir into the fruit mixture. Line a loaf tin with greaseproof paper and brush with the oil. Pour in the fruit mixture and bake at 190°C (375°F), gas mark 5, for 1¼ hours. Cool on a wire rack.

Note Guests and family can eat this loaf spread with butter or margarine if liked, but this is not allowed for in the calories.

Vegetables, Pasta and Rice with Your Meals

Use the following list of handy measures and you can easily dish up your calorie-controlled portion from the dish of vegetables you have cooked for the rest of the family. Where you can count individual items such as a stick of celery, we have given that a calorie value. Where it is necessary to measure, we have used either a 15ml tablespoon or an empty cottage cheese carton (the size which originally held 113g (4 oz) cottage cheese). If you measure in a carton make sure the vegetables are level with the top and are loosely packed.

Asparagus, boiled *or* canned, 5 spears	20
Aubergine, half medium, cooked without fat	15
Baked beans in tomato sauce, per level small cottage cheese carton	115
Baked beans in tomato sauce, per 150-g (5.3-oz) can	110
Baked beans in tomato sauce, per 225-g (7.9-oz) can	160
Beetroot, boiled, per baby beet	5
Beetroot, pickled, per 15ml (1 level tablespoon)	10
Broad beans, boiled *or* canned, per level small cottage cheese carton	50
Broccoli, 2 medium spears	20

Brussels sprouts, boiled *or* frozen, 10 medium
   sprouts   20

Bubble and Squeak, Birds Eye, per patty cooked
   without added fat   50

Butter beans, boiled *or* canned, per level small
   cottage cheese carton   125

Cabbage, raw, shredded, per level small cottage
   cheese carton   10

Cabbage, boiled, per level small cottage cheese
   carton   10

Carrots, sliced and boiled, per level small cottage
   cheese carton   20

Cauliflower, boiled, 1/4 medium cauliflower   15

Celery, raw *or* boiled, 1 stick   5

Courgettes, boiled, 1 medium   10

Courgettes, sliced and fried, 1 medium   40

Cucumber, 2-inch piece   6

Leeks, boiled, 1 medium   25

Lettuce, 1/4 medium   5

Macaroni, brown, boiled, per level small cottage
   cheese carton   95

Macaroni, white, boiled, per level small cottage
   cheese carton   135

Mixed vegetables, frozen, boiled, per level small
   cottage cheese carton   55

Mustard and cress, per whole carton   5

Onions, raw *or* boiled, per medium onion   20

Onions, fried, 15ml (1 level tablespoon)   25

Onions, pickled, 1 medium   5

Onions, cocktail, each   1

Peas, frozen, boiled, per level small cottage
   cheese carton   55

Peas, mushy, per level small cottage cheese carton   145

Peas, processed, canned, per level small cottage cheese carton	105
Pepper, red *or* green, raw *or* boiled, ¼ medium	5
Potatoes, boiled, 1 medium, 125g (4 oz)	90
Potatoes, baked, 1 average jacket potato, 200g (7 oz) raw weight	175
Potatoes, baked, 1 average jacket potato with knob of butter, 15g (½ oz)	280
Potatoes, oven chips, cooked as instructed, per level small cottage cheese carton	110
Potatoes, chips, average thickness, per level small cottage cheese carton	140
Potatoes, mashed with a little milk and butter, per level small cottage cheese carton	185
Potatoes, mashed with a little skimmed milk and no butter, per level small cottage cheese carton	125
Potatoes, roast, 1 medium chunk	75
Potato croquettes, 1 Birds Eye, cooked without added fat	30
Radishes, each	2
Rice, brown, boiled, per level small cottage cheese carton	125
Rice, white, boiled, per level small cottage cheese carton	130
Runner beans, sliced, boiled, per level small cottage cheese carton	25
Spaghetti, white, boiled, per level small cottage cheese carton	130
Spaghetti, wholewheat, boiled, per level small cottage cheese carton	95
Spaghetti, canned in tomato sauce, per level small cottage cheese carton	100

Spaghetti, canned in tomato sauce, per 215-g (7.6-oz) can	140
Spinach, chopped, boiled, per level small cottage cheese carton	35
Spring onions, each	3
Swede, mashed without butter *or* margarine, per level small cottage cheese carton	30
Sweetcorn kernels, boiled, frozen *or* canned, per level small cottage cheese carton	95
Sweetcorn, per average cob, boiled, served without butter	85
Sweetcorn, creamed style, canned, per level small cottage cheese carton	155
Tomatoes, 1 medium	8
Tomatoes, 1 medium halved and fried	40
Tomatoes, 1 medium sliced and fried	60

Calorie Charts

BASIC FOODS

Meat and Poultry

Bacon, back rasher, raw, each	150
Bacon, back rasher, well grilled *or* fried, each	80
Bacon, streaky rasher, raw, each	90
Bacon, streaky rasher, well grilled *or* fried, each	50
Bacon steak, well grilled, 100g (3½ oz) raw weight	105
Beef, brisket, boiled, lean and fat, per 28g (1 oz)	93
Beef, lean ground, raw, per 28g (1 oz)	45
Beef, lean ground, fried and drained of fat, 28g (1 oz) raw weight	40
Beef, minced, raw, per 28g (1 oz)	65
Beef, minced, fried and drained of fat, 28g (1 oz) raw weight	45
Beef, rump steak, well grilled, 170g (6 oz) raw	260
Beef, rump steak, medium grilled, 170g (6 oz) raw	290
Beef, rump steak, rare grilled, 170g (6 oz) raw	310
Beef, stewing steak, raw, lean only, per 28g (1 oz)	35
Beef, topside, roast, lean and fat, per 28g (1 oz)	60
Beef, topside, roast, lean only, per 28g (1 oz)	44
Black pudding, raw, per 28g (1 oz)	78
Brawn, per 28g (1 oz)	43
Chicken, meat only, raw, per 28g (1 oz)	34
Chicken, meat only, boiled, per 28g (1 oz)	52
Chicken, meat only, roast, per 28g (1 oz)	42

Chicken, meat and skin, roast, per 28g (1 oz)	61
Chicken breast, grilled, 170g (6 oz) raw weight	200
Chicken breast, grilled and skin removed, 170g (6 oz) raw weight	145
Chicken drumstick, raw each	90
Chicken drumstick, grilled, each	85
Chicken drumstick, grilled and skin removed, each	65
Chicken leg joint, raw, 227g (8 oz)	410
Chicken leg joint, grilled, 227g (8 oz) raw weight	250
Chicken leg joint, grilled and skin removed, 227g (8 oz) raw weight	165
Duck, roast, meat only, per 28g (1 oz)	54
Duck, roast, meat and skin, per 28g (1 oz)	95
Frankfurter, per 28g (1 oz)	78
Gammon joint, boiled, lean only, per 28g (1 oz)	47
Gammon rashers, grilled, lean and fat, per 28g (1 oz)	67
Gammon rashers, grilled, lean only, per 28g (1 oz)	49
Garlic sausage, per 28g (1 oz)	70
Ham, boiled, lean, per 28g (1 oz)	47
Ham, boiled, fatty, per 28g (1 oz)	90
Haslet, per 28g (1 oz)	80
Heart, lamb's, raw, per 28g (1 oz)	34
Kabanos, per 28g (1 oz)	115
Kidney, all types, raw, per 28g (1 oz)	25
Kidney, per average lamb's kidney, 57g (2 oz)	50
Lamb, breast, boned, roast, lean and fat, per 28g (1 oz)	115
Lamb, leg, roast, lean without bone, per 28g (1 oz)	54
Lamb, leg, roast, lean and fat without bone, per 28g (1 oz)	76
Lamb, shoulder, roast, lean without bone, per 28g (1 oz)	56

Lamb, chump chop, well grilled, 142g (5 oz)
raw weight   205

Lamb, loin chop, well grilled, 142g (5 oz) raw
weight   175

Liver, chicken's, raw, per 28g (1 oz)   38

Liver, lamb's, raw, per 28g (1 oz)   51

Liver, pig's, raw, per 28g (1 oz)   44

Liver sausage, per 28g (1 oz)   88

Luncheon meat, per 28g (1 oz)   89

Pork, fillet, raw, lean only, per 28g (1 oz)   42

Pork, leg, roast, lean and fat, per 28g (1 oz)   81

Pork, leg, roast, lean only, per 28g (1 oz)   53

Pork chop, well grilled, 184g (6½ oz) raw weight   240

Pork crackling, average portion, 9g (⅓ oz)   65

Sausage, beef chipolata, well grilled,
each   50

Sausage, beef, large, well grilled, each   120

Sausage, beef, skinless, well grilled, each   65

Sausage, pork, chipolata, well grilled, each   65

Sausage, pork, large, well grilled, each   125

Sausage, pork, skinless, well grilled, each   95

Sausage, pork and beef, chipolata, well grilled, each   60

Sausage, pork and beef, large, well grilled, each   125

Sausagemeat, raw, per 28g (1 oz)   80

Tongue, lamb's, stewed, per 28g (1 oz)   82

Tongue, ox, boiled, per 28g (1 oz)   83

Turkey, meat only, raw, per 28g (1 oz)   30

Turkey, meat only, roast, per 28g (1 oz)   40

Turkey, meat and skin, roast, per 28g (1 oz)   50

Veal, fillet, raw, per 28g (1 oz)   31

Veal, escalope, fried in egg and breadcrumbs,
85g (3 oz) raw weight   310

Fish

per 28g (1 oz) unless otherwise stated

Anchovies, per fillet	5
Cod, fillet, raw	22
Cod, fillet, baked *or* grilled with a little fat	27
Cod, fillet, fried in batter	57
Cod, fillet, poached in water *or* steamed	24
Coley, fillet, raw	21
Coley, fillet, steamed	28
Haddock fillet, raw	21
Haddock, fillet, fried in breadcrumbs	50
Haddock, smoked fillet, steamed *or* poached in water	29
Halibut, fillet, steamed	37
Halibut, on the bone, raw	26
Halibut, on the bone, steamed	26
Herring, fillet, raw	66
Herring, fillet, grilled	56
Herring, on the bone, grilled	38
Herring, on the bone, fried in oatmeal	59
Herring, rollmop, each	120
Herring, soft roe, raw	23
Kipper, fillet, baked *or* grilled	58
Kipper, per whole kipper, 170g (6 oz)	280
Lemon sole, fillet, steamed *or* poached	26
Mackerel, fillet, raw	63
Mackerel, kippered	62
Mackerel, smoked	70
Pilchards, canned in tomato sauce	36
Plaice, fillet, raw *or* steamed	26
Plaice, whole fillet, fried in breadcrumbs, 142g (5 oz) raw uncrumbed weight	365
Prawns, without shells, fresh *or* frozen	30

Rock salmon, fried in batter	75
Salmon, canned	44
Salmon, fresh, on the bone, steamed	45
Salmon, smoked	40
Sardines, canned in oil, drained	62
Sardines, canned in tomato sauce	50
Scampi, fried in breadcrumbs	90
Shrimps, canned, drained	27
Shrimps, fresh, without shells	33
Trout, whole trout, poached or grilled without fat, 170g (6oz) raw weight	150
Tuna, canned in brine, drained	30
Tuna, canned in oil, drained	60
Tuna, canned in oil, weighed with oil	82
Whitebait, fried	150
Whiting, fillet, fried	54
Whiting, fillet, steamed	26

Vegetables
per 28g (1 oz) unless otherwise stated

Asparagus, raw or boiled	5
Aubergine, raw	4
Beansprouts, canned	3
Beansprouts, raw	5
Beans, butter, boiled	27
Beans, baked, canned in tomato sauce	20
Beans, broad, boiled	14
Beans, red kidney, canned	25
Beans, butter, dry, raw	78
Beans, runner, raw	7
Beetroot, boiled	12
Broccoli, raw	7
Brussels sprouts, raw	7

Cabbage, raw	6
Carrots, raw	6
Cauliflower, raw	4
Celery, one stick	5
Chicory, raw	3
Courgette, raw	4
Courgettes, sliced and fried, 28g (1 oz) raw weight	15
Cucumber	3
Endive, raw	3
Garlic, 1 clove	0
Leeks, raw	9
Lettuce	3
Mushrooms, raw	4
Mushrooms, button, sliced and fried, 57g (2 oz) raw weight	100
Mushrooms, button, fried whole, 57g (2 oz) raw weight	80
Mustard and cress	3
Onions, raw	7
Onions, fried, 15ml (1 level tablespoon)	25
Parsnips, raw	14
Parsnips, roast	30
Peas, fresh, raw	19
Peas, frozen	15
Peas, canned, garden	13
Peas, canned, processed	23
Peppers, red *or* green	4
Plantain, green, raw	30
Potatoes, raw	25
Potatoes, baked, weighed with skin	24
Potatoes, boiled, old potatoes	24
Potatoes, boiled, new potatoes	23
Potatoes, chips, average thickness	70

Potatoes, chips, crinkle cut	80
Potatoes, chips, thick cut	40
Potatoes, chips, thin cut	85
Potatoes, mashed with milk and butter	35
Potatoes, roast, medium chunks	45
Potatoes, sauté	40
Radishes, whole medium radish	2
Spinach, boiled	9
Spring greens, boiled	1
Spring onions, each	3
Swede, raw	6
Swede, boiled	5
Sweetcorn, canned in brine	22
Sweetcorn, frozen	25
Sweet potato, raw	32
Sweet potato, boiled	24
Tomatoes, raw	4
Tomatoes, canned	3
Turnips, raw	6
Turnips, boiled	4
Watercress	4

Eggs

each	Raw	Fried
Size 1	95	115
Size 2	90	110
Size 3	80	100
Size 4	75	95
Size 5	70	90

Cheese
per 28g (1 oz) unless otherwise stated

Blue Stilton	131

Brie	88
Camembert	88
Cheddar	120
Cheese spread, plain *or* flavoured	80
Cheese spread, per triangle, 14g (½ oz)	40
Cheshire	110
Cottage cheese	27
Cream cheese	125
Curd cheese	40
Danish blue	103
Double Gloucester	105
Edam	88
Gouda	100
Lancashire	109
Leicester	105
Parmesan	118
Parmesan, grated, per 15ml (1 level tablespoon)	30
Philadelphia	90
Processed	88
1 Kraft Processed Cheese Cheddar Singles Slice	65
Riccotta	55
Skimmed Milk Soft Cheese	25
Wensleydale	115

Milk
per 568ml (1 pint) unless otherwise stated

Channel Island *or* Gold Top	430
Condensed, full-fat, sweetened, per 28g (1 oz)	91
Evaporated, full fat milk, per 28g (1 oz)	45
Homogenized *or* Red Top	370
Instant spray dried skimmed milk, reconstituted	200
Instant dried skimmed milk, dry, 15ml (1 level tablespoon)	18

Instant dried skimmed milk with vegetable fat, reconstituted	280
UHT *or* Longlife	370
Pasteurized *or* Silver Top	370
Skimmed *or* separated	200
Sterilized	370

Cream
per 15ml (1 level tablespoon)

Clotted	105
Double	60
Half	20
Single	30
Soured	30
Sterilized, canned	35
Whipping	45

Yogurt
per 28g (1 oz)

Low-fat, natural	15
Low-fat, flavoured	23
Low-fat, fruit	27

Fats and Oils

Butter, 28g (1 oz)	210
Butter, 5ml (1 level teaspoon)	35
Cooking and salad oil, all types, 15ml (1 level tablespoon)	120
Dripping, 15ml (1 level tablespoon)	125
Lard, 28g (1 oz)	253
Low-fat spread, all brands, 28g (1 oz)	105
Low-fat spread, all brands, 5ml (1 level teaspoon)	20
Margarine, all brands, 28g (1 oz)	210

Margarine, all brands, 5ml (1 level teaspoon)   35
Solid vegetable oil, 28g (1 oz)   255
Shredded suet, 28g (1 oz)   235

Bread, Rolls, Buns etc.
Brown *or* wheatmeal bread, medium slice from
  a large loaf   80
Bap, 50g (1³/₄ oz)   130
Bread stick, each   15
Chelsea bun, 92g (3¹/₄ oz)   255
Croissant, 57g (2 oz)   220
Crumpet, 42g (1¹/₂ oz)   75
Crusty roll, brown *or* white, 50g (1³/₄ oz)   145
Currant bread, 1 small slice, 28g (1 oz)   70
French bread, 57g (2 oz) piece   130
Hovis roll, 45g (1⁵/₈ oz)   115
Malt bread, 1 small slice, 28g (1 oz)   70
Soft brown roll, 50g (1³/₄ oz)   140
Soft white roll, 50g (1³/₄ oz)   155
Tea cake, 57g (2 oz)   155
Wheatgerm bread, e.g., Hovis and Vitbe, per
  medium slice from a large, sliced loaf   80
White bread, per medium slice from a large,
  sliced loaf   85
White bread, per thick slice from a large, sliced
  loaf   90
White bread, per thin slice from a large, sliced loaf   60
Wholemeal bread, 28g (1 oz)   61
Wholemeal roll, 45g (1³/₄ oz)   125

Cereal Products
per 28g (1 oz) unless otherwise stated
Barley, Pearl, raw   102

Barley, Pearl, boiled	34
Bran	58
Cornflour	100
Cornflour, per 15ml (1 level tablespoon)	33
Flour, wheatmeal	93
Flour, white plain	99
Flour, white self-raising	96
Flour, wholemeal	90
Muesli	105
Oatmeal, raw	114
Sago, raw	101
Semolina, raw	99
Tapioca, raw	102
Wheatgerm	100

Pasta and Rice
per 28g (1 oz)

Macaroni, raw	105
Macaroni, boiled	33
Pasta, all shapes, raw	105
Pasta, all shapes, boiled	33
Rice, brown, raw	95
Rice, brown, boiled	35
Rice, white, raw	103
Rice, white, boiled	35
Spaghetti, white, raw	107
Spaghetti, white, boiled	33
Spaghetti, wholewheat, raw	97
Spaghetti, canned in tomato sauce	17

Sauces/Pickles
per 15ml (1 level tablespoon)

Apple sauce, sweetened	20

Apple sauce, unsweetened   10
Branston *or* Ploughman's pickle   20
Bread sauce   15
Brown sauce   15
Cranberry sauce   45
French dressing   75
Horseradish   13
Low-calorie salad cream   25
Mango chutney   35
Mayonnaise   95
Mint sauce   5
Oil-free French Dressing   3
Parsley sauce   45
Salad Cream   50
Soy sauce   13
Tartare sauce   35
Tomato ketchup   15
Worcestershire sauce   13

Fruit, Fresh, Canned and Dried
Apple, medium whole eating apple, 142g (5 oz)   50
Apple, medium whole cooking apple, 227g (8 oz)   80
Apricots, canned in natural juice, per 28g (1 oz)   13
Apricots, canned in syrup, per 28g (1 oz)   30
Apricots, dried, each   10
Apricots, fresh, each, 28g (1 oz)   7
Banana, small whole fruit, 142g (5 oz)   65
Banana, medium whole fruit, 170g (6 oz)   80
Banana, large whole fruit, 198g (7 oz)   95
Blackberries, raw, per 28g (1 oz)   8
Blackcurrants, raw, per 28g (1 oz)   8
Cherries, fresh with stones, per 28g (1 oz)   12
Cherries, glacé, each   10

Currants, per 28g (1 oz)	69
Currants, per 15ml (1 level tablespoon)	25
Damsons, fresh with stones, per 28g (1 oz)	10
Dates, dried without stones, per 28g (1 oz)	70
Gooseberries, fresh cooking, per 28g (1 oz)	5
Grapefruit, fresh, half of medium fruit, 170g (6 oz)	20
Grapefruit, canned in natural juice, per 28g (1 oz)	11
Grapefruit, canned in sugar, per 28g (1 oz)	17
Grapes, black, per 28g (1 oz)	11
Grapes, white, per 28g (1 oz)	17
Lemon, medium whole fruit, 142g (5 oz)	20
Lychees, canned, per 28g (1 oz)	19
Mandarins, canned in syrup, per 28g (1 oz)	16
Mandarin, fresh, per whole medium fruit, 70g (2½ oz)	20
Melon, Canteloupe, Honeydew *or* Yellow, per 227-g (8-oz) slice	32
Oranges, whole, small fruit, 142g (5 oz)	35
Orange, whole medium fruit, 227g (8 oz)	55
Orange, whole large fruit, 284g (10 oz)	75
Peaches, canned in syrup, per 28g (1 oz)	25
Peaches, canned in natural juice, per 28g (1 oz)	13
Peaches, fresh, per whole medium fruit, 113g (4 oz)	35
Pears, canned in syrup, per 28g (1 oz)	22
Pears, canned in natural juice, per 28g (1 oz)	11
Pears, fresh, per whole medium fruit, 142g (5 oz)	40
Pineapple, canned in syrup, per ring, drained	35
Pineapple, fresh, flesh only, per 28g (1 oz)	13
Plums, cooking, per 28g (1 oz)	7
Plums, dessert, per 28g (1 oz)	10
Plums, Victoria dessert, per whole medium fruit	15
Prunes, each	10
Raisins, per 28g (1 oz)	70

Raisins, per 15ml (1 level tablespoon)	25
Raspberries, fresh *or* frozen, per 28g (1 oz)	7
Rhubarb, raw, per 28g (1 oz)	2
Rhubarb, stewed without sugar, per 28g (1 oz)	2
Strawberries, fresh, per 28g (1 oz)	7
Sultanas, per 28g (1 oz)	71
Sultanas, per 15ml (1 level tablespoon)	25
Tangerines, whole medium fruit, 70g (2½ oz)	20
Watermelon, per 28g (1 oz)	3

Nuts
per 28g (1 oz)

Almonds, shelled	160
Barcelona, shelled	181
Beech, shelled	160
Brazil, shelled	176
Cashew, shelled	160
Chestnuts, shelled	48
Cob, shelled	108
Coconut flesh, fresh	100
Coconut, dessicated	172
Hazelnuts, shelled	108
Peanuts, dry roasted	160
Peanuts, fresh, shelled	162
Peanuts, roasted, salted	168
Peanut butter	177
Pistachio, shelled	180
Walnuts, shelled	149

Sweet Biscuits
per average biscuit

Bourbon cream	65
Chocolate Coated Digestive	70

Custard cream	60
Digestive, small	45
Digestive, medium	55
Digestive, large	70
Fig roll	65
Garibaldi, finger	30
Ginger nut	40
Ginger snap	35
Lincoln	10
Malted milk	40
Marie	30
Morning coffee	25
Nice	45
Oatmeal thrifty	35
Petit beurre	30
Rich Tea, finger	25
Rich Tea, round	45
Rich Osborne	35
Sponge finger	20
Thin arrowroot	30

Savoury Biscuits
per average biscuit

Cheese cracker	20
Cheese football	15
Cheese sandwich	50
Cornish wafer	50
Cream cracker	35
Hovis cracker	30
Water biscuit	30

Spreads, Preserves, Sugar
per 5ml (1 level teaspoon)

Chocolate spread	20
Honey	18
Jam	17
Lemon curd	13
Low-calorie vegetable spread	5
Marmalade	17
Marmite	10
Mincemeat	13
Molasses	15
Peanut butter	35
Redcurrant jelly	15
Sugar, white and brown	17
Syrup, golden	20
Syrup, maple	17
Treacle, black	17

Chocolates/Sweets
per 28g (1 oz)

Barley sugar	100
Boiled sweets	95
Butterscotch	115
Chocolate, milk *or* plain	150
Chocolates, filled	130
Fudge	110
Liquorice allsorts	105
Marshmallows	90
Nougat	110
Peppermints	110
Toffee	122

DRINKS

Soft Drinks and Beverages

Apple juice, per 28ml (1 fl. oz)	10
Coffee, black	0
Cola, one can (11½ fl. oz)	125
Cocoa, per rounded teaspoon (10ml)	20
Drinking chocolate, per rounded teaspoon (10ml)	20
Grapefruit juice, unsweetened, per 28ml (1 fl. oz)	8
Grapefruit juice, sweetened, per 28ml (1 fl. oz)	11
Lemonade, one can (11½ fl. oz)	70
Orange juice, unsweetened, per 28ml (1 fl. oz)	11
Orange juice, sweetened, per 28ml (1 fl. oz)	15
Orange squash, 45ml (3 tablespoons)	35
Pineapple juice, per 28ml (1 fl. oz)	15
Tea, no milk	0
Tomato juice, per 28ml (1 fl. oz)	6

Alcoholic Drinks

Wines
per average glass, 113ml (4 fl. oz)

Dry red	80
Dry white	75
Rosé	80
Sparkling white, including champagne	90
Sweet red	95
Sweet white	100

Spirits
per pub measure, 25ml (⅙ gill)

Brandy, Whisky, Gin, Rum and Vodka	50

Sherry and Port
per small schooner, 50ml (1/3 gill)

Dry sherry	55
Medium sherry	60
Cream sherry	65
Port	75

Apéritifs and Vermouths
per pub measure 50ml (1/3 gill)

Campari	115
Cinzano Bianco	80
Cinzano Rosso	75
Dubonnet Dry	55
Dubonnet Red	75
Martini Bianco	75
Martini Extra Dry	55
Martini Rosé and Rosso	80
Noilly Dry French	55

Beer and Cider
per 283ml (1/2 pint)

Dry cider	105
Lager	85
Low-carbohydrate Lager	80
Light Ale	75
Shandy	75
Stout	105
Sweet Cider	120
Vintage Cider	180

Index

Index

Fontana Paperbacks: Non-fiction

Fontana is a leading paperback publisher of non-fiction, both popular and academic. Below are some recent titles.

☐ THE POLITICS OF INDUSTRIAL RELATIONS (second edition) Colin Crouch £2·95
☐ NATTER NATTER Richard Briers £1·50
☐ KITCHEN HINTS Hilary Davies £1·25
☐ MRS WEBER'S DIARY Posy Simmonds £2·50
☐ A TREASURY OF CHRISTMAS Frank & Jamie Muir £2·95
☐ THE VIDEO HANDBOOK John Baxter & Brian Norris £1·95
☐ A BOOK OF SEA JOURNEYS Ludovic Kennedy (ed.) £3·50
☐ BEDSIDE GOLF Peter Alliss £1·95
☐ DAY CARE Alison Clarke-Stewart £1·95
☐ THE WOMAN QUESTION: READINGS ON THE SUBORDINATION OF WOMEN Mary Evans (ed.) £3·95
☐ WAR FACTS NOW Christy Campbell £2·50
☐ CHRONICLE OF YOUTH Vera Brittain £2·75
☐ FRIGHTENED FOR MY LIFE Geoff Coggan & Martin Walker £1·95
☐ HIGH PRESSURE: WORKING LIVES OF WOMEN MANAGERS Cary Cooper & Marilyn Davidson £1·95
☐ TRADE UNIONS: THE LOGIC OF COLLECTIVE ACTION Colin Crouch £2·50
☐ THE KINGDOM Robert Lacey £2·95
☐ A FOREIGN FLAVOUR Rose Elliot £2·95
☐ SEVEN DAYS TO DISASTER Des Hickey & Gus Smith £2·50
☐ P.S. I LOVE YOU Michael Sellers £1·75

You can buy Fontana paperbacks at your local bookshop or newsagent. Or you can order them from Fontana Paperbacks, Cash Sales Department, Box 29, Douglas, Isle of Man. Please send a cheque, postal or money order (not currency) worth the purchase price plus 10p per book (or plus 12p per book if outside the UK).

NAME (Block letters) _____

ADDRESS _____

_____

_____